SOME WORDS IN ADVANCE

Janice Barnhart's suggestions for preventive discipline are easy to understand, simple to apply and very effective in their results. Examples of day to day situations familiar to any parent are clear and easy to adapt.

Her empathy for both the busy parent and the growing child shines through her writing. She approaches the reader with the same caring respect and understanding that she advocates in her chapters on preventive discipline.

Carol Hardgrove, M.A.
Counseling and Early Childhood Education

In reading *Preventive Discipline* one feels comfortably engaged in a personal consultation not only with an experienced parent, but with an astute observer and a sensitive, caring and nurturing person with a talent for articulate expression of practical guidelines for child rearing. With my own children now grown, I realize we all would have benefited by having this roadmap in hand when they were still toddlers.

Jerome A. Motto, M.D.
Professor of Psychiatry, Emeritus
University of California at San Francisco

Throughout this wise little book on preventive discipline, Janice Barnhart shows how positive attention, respect, and sympathetic understanding can weave a strong fabric of positive parent-child interactions. She offers realistic advice from one who has been there and faced the day-to-day challenges of building a supportive family. This book is realistic, emphasizing the practical and the possible.

This book is timely, written as we look within ourselves for reliable ways to keep families together, keep them strong, and rear healthy, competent children.

This book is inspiring. Janice Barnhart's words make me wish I could try some of it over again, do it better, and enjoy it more in the process!

Tynette Hills, Ph.D.
Consultant, Early Childhood Education

PREVENTIVE

DISCIPLINE

A ROAD MAP FOR GOOD BEHAVIOR
FROM TODDLER TO TEEN

by

JANICE S. BARNHART

Illustrations by Dorothy Messenger

Printed in the United States of America

ISBN: 0-9654940-0-4

Library of Congress Catalog Card Number: 96-94978

Cover Design: Allen Crider, Fairfax, CA
Photography: Randy Silver, San Carlos, CA
Printing: Patterson Printing, Benton Harbor, MI
Typesetting and Styling: Jeannine Feldman, San Mateo, CA

To my husband, Don,
and my children,
Fred, Becky and Julie,
without whom I would never have written this book

TABLE OF CONTENTS

PREFACE

Most people want to have children in order to carry on the family name and values, to share their day-to-day lives, and to provide a kind of immortality. But too often people find child rearing a heavy burden. I believe it can be a joy. I am writing this book because I want to share a philosophy of child rearing which I developed over the years—one which, I believe, brings joy.

The ideas in this book are an outgrowth of my experiences as a child, mother and teacher. To explain briefly, I was a child in two families, one with my stepmother and biological father, the other with my biological mother and stepfather. Their different styles of child rearing left me with insights I could get no other way. In addition, I had the experience of raising three children of my own, a son and twin daughters. Further, as a parent, I read extensively on child development and arranged for a number of parent education programs while a member of civic organizations such as the PTA (Parent/Teacher Association) and AAUW (American Association of University Women.) My experience in teaching was principally with special education students, as a private tutor and aide, and as a home teacher in the elementary grades in the San Bruno Park (California) School District. I was also head of the Tutoring Center at Peninsula High School (a continuation school in San Mateo County, California), adding a further dimension. This variety of experiences has helped me develop the philosophy I wish to share with you.

I want to point out that our children were raised in the '50s and '60s, when fathers did not take as prominent a part as they do now. However, my husband was more involved than the majority of fathers at that time. Very important then, as now, we agreed on the general philosophy of child rearing and family values. I should also like to emphasize that, in my opinion, the ideas I put forth on discipline in my book are valid for whomever the care giver of the child is, whether it be mother, father or child care provider.

Let me say that by no means did I apply my ideas successfully at all times. No parent can be insightful, consistent, and clear thinking every minute of every day. Rather, my message is that the more I followed this philosophy, the more successful I was in having well behaved, happy children.

I hope that my sharing these ideas will help you to develop approaches that work for you. My fondest hope is that you will find the important job of child rearing both joyful and rewarding.

ACKNOWLEDGMENTS

Even though I put an enormous amount of time and effort into writing this book, I could never have done it without the invaluable help of a number of family members and friends. I should like to acknowledge and thank them for their contributions.

First, I wish to thank my immediate family. My husband, Don, not only gave me encouragement and support, but also let me use our word processor a lion's share of the time; our twin daughters, Becky and Julie, showed great interest in my progress and sent me material which was helpful; and Fred and Dede, my son and his wife, read and critiqued the first draft to give it a reality check for the '90s.

Second, I am lucky to have a cousin, Neysa Hebbard, an editor for several publishers before her retirement, who agreed to look over my manuscript. Her seasoned eye has been most valuable and appreciated.

Finally, two longtime friends have made very important contributions. Dorothy Messenger, a friend since college days who was always clever with line drawings, agreed to do the illustrations. I believe they capture the essence of the text. Another friend, Carol Gerk, who has taught a child observation class for pre-schoolers for some years, both commented on my first draft and engaged me for several talks to the parents of children in her class.

To all these people, I give my heartfelt thanks and gratitude.

THE BASICS:
AN INTRODUCTION

The word discipline brings different images to different people. To some it means scolding or punishing. To others it means constantly giving orders. Still others consider discipline as a way of relating constructively to children in order to get the behavior wanted. This last is my concept of discipline and what I want to share in this book.

I believe that the most effective way to inspire good behavior in children is through preventive discipline—a way of interacting with children that prevents most misbehavior and provides a means of dealing with the inevitable misbehavior that does occur.

Children—whether infants, toddlers, elementary school-age children or teenagers—have basic needs. There are the obvious physical needs for food, shelter and rest, and the more subtle psychological needs for love, approval and belonging. These psychological needs are not always as easy to recognize or meet, but are just as important. Satisfying children's basic needs, both physical and psychological, are the keystones to forming a solid base for good behavior.

There is little disagreement about the physical needs of children, although we need constantly to remind ourselves to consider them in our daily scheduling. All too often we forget that a child may get tired and hungry before we do, especially when we are shopping or traveling. When we do forget, we often end up with a fussy or misbehaving child. Consciously thinking about these physical needs can help us fulfill them quite adequately.

Meeting the psychological needs of children is quite another matter. There are many theories about what these needs are, how to satisfy them, and how all this relates to good behavior.

The cornerstone of this book on preventive discipline is my belief that relating to children in a way that satisfies their psychological needs—assuming their physical needs are met—can inspire the kind of behavior we want and prevent most misbehavior.

Children have a strong urge to have their basic psychological needs met, and they will go to great lengths to be sure they get what they need. Sometimes they resort to negative behavior, usually called misbehavior. They will demand attention if they are not getting enough, and they often rebel against lack of respect or understanding. Some children show their negative behavior by withdrawing instead of acting out. Such withdrawal can be hard to think of as misbehavior, because the apathy sometimes shown can look like good behavior. However, it is just as much a signal that something is amiss. Changing our approach to discipline can change both kinds of misbehavior—acting out and withdrawal—into good behavior.

In the first part of the book, I spell out what I mean by preventive discipline by describing in some detail what I believe are its basic elements: attention, respect and empathy. I include specific examples of dialogue and other interactions between parent and child to illustrate how to put these elements into action in our relations with our children to achieve good behavior. In these examples I alternate "she" and "he," since we are as concerned with girls' behavior as with boys'. Of course all examples apply to either sex.

Part two of the book goes into more specific ways to help avoid misbehavior, as well as ways to deal with the inevitable misbehavior that does occur. Among specific problems dealt with are eating and sleeping problems and anger, including temper tantrums.

Part three offers ideas on approaching a number of situations that often lead to conflicts between parents and children, such as homework, TV and money. Again, the three elements of preventive discipline are the keys to avoiding or solving such problems.

The fourth and final part of the book offers some closing thoughts. I urge parents to be patient as they practice preventive discipline, for it takes time for both parents and children to overcome old patterns. Also I emphasize again the importance of considering a child's maturity level, as well as our own limitations, in our efforts to achieve success as parents. I conclude with the theme "happiness is expecting the possible."

In the Appendix, I share a list of "Be-Attitudes" which have been helpful to me in relating to my own children and grandchildren, and which I hope will be helpful to my readers as well. Also included is a description of family games we have played when traveling, to help the time pass more happily. Finally, I have listed some books for suggested reading.

To sum up, preventive discipline—as reflected in this book—is built on the idea that we can influence good behavior in our children and deal with any misbehavior by being aware of their basic needs and meeting them. These are really human needs, and satisfying them in our relationships with all people—children and adults alike—can avoid many conflicts and confrontations, making for a smoother and happier life for everyone.

PART ONE

PAVING STONES TO GOOD BEHAVIOR

1

ATTENTION

Attention is the first essential element in preventive discipline. By attention I mean our response to a child's being with us, our response to her interests and comments and questions without being preoccupied or thinking about something else. This kind of attention, which I call positive attention, is the only kind that works.

How much attention is enough? Observing our children is a good gauge of that. If they get the amount of positive attention they need, they quit demanding it. The exception might be the child who has received a tremendous amount of attention and stimulation which we might see with a first child. She may have a hard time being satisfied with less time when it has to be shared with siblings as they come along. Deciding on how much attention is enough is a matter of judgment. An approach is to encourage the first child to spend some time entertaining herself, to be self sufficient, even when you as the parent have time and energy to spare.

In my own family, I found that giving the amount of attention wanted by my three children was not too hard when I was around, but if I was out too many nights to meetings, my son would become quite mischievous. It was not serious misbehavior, just annoying.

By cutting back on nights out, all was back to normal. Even though their dad was home to give them good attention, the children seemed to think that a certain minimum was my job as the mother.

Of course, I realize that in today's world, with so many mothers working, it is not possible to be as flexible as I could be. Nevertheless, arrangements for good child care and a routine that can be counted on is of paramount importance in supplementing the child's need for positive attention.

Distractions Which Can Inhibit Good Attention

Preoccupation

We all have lots on our minds. We may be preoccupied or lost in thought about what to have for dinner, how to ask the boss for a raise, what to wear to the company party, and a myriad of other concerns. But children are not satisfied with absent-minded "ums" and "uh-huhs." They keep doing things to get our attention. For example, if we are shopping and thinking about what to have for dinner, we can say, "What'll we have for a vegetable? These zucchini look good. Shall we get some?" Such exchanges offer a good chance to turn our concern into an attentive chat, and of course the children may come up with some good suggestions.

Another thing to remember is that children are not *always* with us. They take naps, go to bed before we do, are at preschool, or playing with friends. If we can save our doing and thinking about things in which children are not interested until they are not around, we can give positive attention when they are with us. They will be more content and so will we.

Talking to our children as we would to a friend is a fine guideline for good, positive attention. For example, how would we answer a friend when she makes a comment or asks a question? We use words and body language that show we really care. This kind of response is necessary for a good friendship, and it is also necessary for contented children. I will always remember one mother's response when I was giving a program: "If we talked to our friends as we do to our children, we wouldn't have any friends!"

Talking On the Telephone

Talking on the Telephone
We all know how our children can behave when we talk on the telephone; they often start wanting a lot of attention. Having a toy telephone handy helps for a few minutes, but then the demands begin all over. Saying,

"Let me talk for just a minute," did not work at all for me. What *did* work was letting the children say hello to friends, and then keeping the conversation short. Business calls were short enough that the toy telephones were sufficient.

How we would relate if a friend were visiting was a helpful guide for me. Would we have a long conversation? If we did so, the friend would feel excluded and a bit hurt. We would probably keep the conversation short and call back later. This would be in the best interests of our friendship, and the same behavior goes a long way toward satisfying a child when we are on the phone.

Chatting With A Friend in Person

What happens when we take our child shopping and meet a friend in the supermarket? If the conversation is longer than a hello and a few bits of news, the child usually begins tugging at our sleeve, interrupting the conversation, or banging the basket. She cannot take being excluded for long. Of course, she does need to learn not to interrupt. We can say, "Please don't interrupt while I'm talking," but we need to either cut the conversation short or include her very soon. When I took my young twins shopping and met a friend, I would say something like, "Girls, you remember Mrs. Hall. She's David's mother." That would set the stage for making them feel included, but it still would not be satisfying for very long.

As a guideline, think of what you would do if you went to the store with a friend and met another friend. You would include her in the conversation or make it very short, getting back quickly to the first friend. Children and friends respond well to the same kind of treatment.

Conditions That Keep Parents From Giving Enough Positive Attention

Being Busy Or Tired

As is so often the case, my children wanted attention or asked questions when I was very busy or tired. The temptation was to say, "Don't bother me," or "I'm busy now," but I found that my children would not give up. The result: we all became frustrated.

Timing is very important. Children need a positive response the moment they need it. I discovered that it was easier (and did not take any more time) to give a short answer than to try to put them off. For example, my young son asked, "How do bees make honey?" Having learned my lesson, I took a deep breath and answered, "They take the sweet liquid from flowers and turn it into honey in the beehive." He was not satisfied with the short answer, so I added, "We'll talk more about it after dinner." Then I followed through. I knew that if I did not, I would have a hard time getting by with a short answer next time. Of course if I could turn them over to their dad at these times, which I often did if he was home, it helped satisfy the need for attention.

Being A Working Mother

Having two jobs—wage earner and homemaker— is a heavy load. By the time you get out of work, do the shopping, pick up the children and get home, you are exhausted. Groceries need to be put away, dinner needs to be prepared. To top it off, the children demand attention; a daily crisis is in the making.

Here is a solution to try. Forget all the chores for five to ten minutes when you get home and give the children your undivided attention. It can be a good time for a snack, a cup of tea for you and milk for the children. You get renewed energy, and it gives you a chance to listen and respond to the children's excited tales of the day's happenings, both good and bad. Everyone feels refreshed and satisfied. You are behind very little in time, but way ahead in contentment. Also, you are establishing a tradition of good communication.

This idea works well for the busy, weary non-working mom too!

Rewards of Good Positive Attention

Counteracting Boredom in Children

Attention is one of our best allies in counteracting boredom in young children. They have very short attention spans and need something to keep them interested. Talking with them helps keep their interest. If we are waiting somewhere for a short time, we can show children signs, pictures, animals—anything we see. If a long wait is coming up, as in the doctor's office, we can be prepared with books, toys, crayons. Such diversions provide a chance to have a good time with our child as well as fight boredom; since there is nothing we can do but wait, anyway, we might as well make good use of the time. I found that a wait in the doctor's office was a chance to have some undivided time with my children—often hard to arrange in a busy schedule.

Building A Feeling of Belonging And A Good Self Image

There are several important needs that are fulfilled by positive attention. Children feel loved and approved of and develop a feeling of belonging when we respond to their comments, answer their questions, and admire their accomplishments.

According to a close friend who has been a preschool teacher for years, a child's feeling of belonging is of critical importance. Children who have behavior problems—whether they be acting out or withdrawing—often give signals that they lack this important feeling of belonging.

It is largely a self image problem and permeates all their relationships. Good positive attention, along with respect for the individual (discussed at length in the next section), helps create these all-important feelings.

Observing other Mothers or Care Givers

One of the most valuable college assignments I ever had after I was a mother myself was to watch how other mothers or care givers related to their children in various situations. I was to write down everything that happened, including the words spoken. It was an eye-opener. I recommend it for everyone. You can do this informally as you shop or are in any situation where you can observe mothers, or other care givers, and their children. I saw at first hand what works and what does not, in the best lab of all—the real world. It was this experience that make me a true believer in positive attention, because I noticed that the children who had the attention they needed were well-behaved and happy, while those who did not were constantly misbehaving and being scolded or yelled at. I urge you to watch others and see what happens.

Following are some of the most memorable observations I made. (The comments in parentheses are mine.)

Mother and son, about 8, in grocery store

The boy banged the basket against the checkout counter as he and his mother waited in line. The mother absentmindedly looked off into space. When the banging got bad, she snapped at the child, "Quit that," then looked off again in a preoccupied manner. The child stopped for a moment, then started again until the mother looked at him and said angrily, "Didn't I tell you to stop that?" (Negative attention, to the child, appeared better than none at all.)

Mother pushing daughter, about 5, in grocery cart

Mother and child looked relaxed and were chatting with each other. The mother, as she picked out fruit, said, "I'll get some oranges. They look good. Would you like some apples?" "Yes, and some bananas too." After that they rolled on by, still talking amiably to each other. (Grocery shopping seemed to be a pleasant task for both of them.)

Boy, about 4, in doctor's office with mother and her friend

Mother and her friend were having an animated conversation while the child sat on the floor, building with little blocks. When he finished a structure he would say, "Look, Mom." His mother would turn her head toward him, smile and nod, then go back to talking to her friend. This happened several times. (What surprised me was that an approving look and nod were enough to satisfy the child. The mother did not have to break her conversation to says something like, "Good," or "How nice.")

Mother and two pre-schoolers in line at post office

The children, a girl, about three, and a boy, about five, soon got tired of standing quietly by their mother, who was lost in thought. They started hanging onto the rope dividers for the queue. Before long a metal standard holding the rope fell over with a loud clatter, the little girl falling down with it. "Stand up. Don't knock that over!" the mother said in an irritated voice. She gave the girl a slap on the bottom that made her cry. The boy ran to a chair in the corner and climbed on it. The little girl joined him and then they began running around the post office. The embarrassed mother yelled at them, "Stop that and come over here!" They came for a few seconds, then started running again.

(It was certainly a difficult situation, but positive attention could have helped. There were several animal posters, a flag, several signs, and an automatic door—all items that could have provided topics for useful discussion. For example, they could have talked about the animals, the colors of the flag, the letters in the signs, and they could have counted the number of people who came through the automatic door.)

The Older Child

My comments throughout this section have been about young children and how we, as parents, relate to them. However, I want to emphasize that as children grow older into school age and the teens, they still have the same needs—to be approved of, to be loved, and to have a feeling of belonging. Positive attention continues to be a main essential in satisfying these needs, even though the demands are different.

Satisfying older children's need for attention is not a full time job because they are not with us as much of the time. On the other hand, older children are more demanding because their thoughts and questions are more advanced and need an even greater portion of our best thought and attention. If they do not get it, they will go where they can get the attention they crave. This can lead to many of the problems we hear of between teenagers and parents.

I think of one girlfriend with whom I went to high school who said she could not talk to her mother about what was bothering her because her mother, a teacher, was too busy and tired. She confided in me and another girl-friend. I remember another girl who could only "talk" to the parent of a friend, and still another who confided in a favorite teacher. Whether any of us confidants give the kind of advice or support the parent would have wished is highly questionable. I was grateful that my mother had time and energy to listen to me when I needed to talk.

In conclusion, positive attention is a necessary part of a good relationship, no matter what the ages of the persons involved. It works with young and older children—and adults as well.

2

RESPECT

We can all agree that adults need and demand respect to be productive and happy. Children, too, need respect for the same reasons, and it is therefore a necessary element of preventive discipline. Children not only need respect, they misbehave in some way if they do not get it. Respect is necessary for developing a good self image and a feeling of worth. This need is very strong, and children will fight to get it. It's a matter of self defense. The most helpful guideline in showing respect is to treat our children as we would a friend. We have already developed the choice of words, tone of voice and body language we use with our friends, so the model is in place. Children are much happier to do as asked if we ask respectfully. I do not mean pleadingly; simple respect is sufficient. That makes disciplining easier. We do not order our friends around. We suggest or direct in a positive way in order to get cooperation. The same method works with children.

When we teach our children new behavior instead of asking them to do something they know how to do, we are often on unfamiliar ground. Teaching and learning new behavior can be difficult. *A helpful model here is good employer to employee relations.* When we think about what we like most in being trained for a new job, some things on which we can agree are: (1) clear instructions before starting, (2) understanding from the boss if we get confused or forget, (3) correction that does not humiliate and, preferably, is out of earshot of our co workers, (4) appreciation for good work, and (5) respectful tone and choice of words throughout. The same things work in training or disciplining children. They learn what is wanted and are able to do the job, feeling good about themselves in the process. Everybody wins. The child learns what is expected and both parent and child feel successful.

There are a number of important ways we can show respect for our children. Following are ten I especially want to emphasize:

1. stress cooperation instead of obedience
2. use "I" and "we" messages
3. consider a child's age and development
4. accentuate the positive
5. keep crystal clear
6. stay open-minded
7. be non-judgmental
8. answer questions in a serious way
9. respect a child's space, and
10. insist on respect for a parent's space, too

Stressing Cooperation Instead Of Obedience

If we think of good behavior in children as cooperation instead of obedience, we have taken a big step toward showing respect. In cooperation, we ask a person to do something; in obedience, we demand that they do it. Which do we adults respond to best? Being asked shows respect and makes us want to please; being told or ordered makes us resentful and can even make us rebel against something perfectly logical and simple. Children are amazingly like adults in this way.

Asking a child to do something in a respectful way can still be strong and authoritative. It does not mean we let a child do as he pleases. It means that we use a different choice of words and tone of voice to get the behavior we want.

Some ideas that work are—

The suggestion	**Instead of**
Let's get in the car.	Get in the car.
Time to wash your hands.	Wash your hands.

The "could" question	**Instead of**
Could you hold this for me?	Here—hold this.
Could you stand here out of the way?	Get out of the way.

The simple observation	**Instead of**
There's some food on your mouth.	Wipe your mouth.
It's too noisy in here.	Be quiet.

My suggestion in each example stays away from the direct order, though I have seen that work for some parents. In those cases, I noticed that they used a tone of voice and body language that they would use with friends. Their tone of voice was respectful, so they got cooperation from their children. The way we talk and act makes all the difference in whether the statement comes across as a direction or an order.

As an exercise, let's imagine how we would say each of the following statements, first to a child, and then to a friend:

"Sit here by me."
"Hand me your plate."
"Pass the salt."
"Come over here."

For most of us, there was probably quite a difference between the two ways of saying the same thing. If that was the case, for best results we could practice softening the demands to our children. Adding a phrase such as "How about. . ." or "Please. . ." in front of statements that sound like demands is one way of accomplishing this.

Unfortunately, it is all too easy for us as parents to get in the habit of making demands using the tone of voice and body language of a sergeant giving orders to a recruit. Using more respectful messages gives the child a chance to feel that he has some control over his actions— a strong desire in a child. This approach gives him a chance to think, Yes, I'll do that. Often the positive response is not immediate, so it is wise to be patient and wait a moment for the desired response. The reaction to being curtly ordered about is to feel like a non-person with no control. It is no wonder that there is often strong resistance.

Even young children who cannot yet talk can understand the approach I have outlined. They understand many more words than we realize, and they easily pick up the spirit in which we speak—both through tone of voice and body language. For example, when my son was about 18 months old, he wanted to get out of his stroller and walk when we were coming home from the grocery store. I had a bag of groceries in the back of the stroller and needed his weight to balance it. I said, "I need you to ride in the stroller to balance the groceries. We'll take a walk after we get home." Fortunately, he sat back down and rode the rest of the way.

If we give our children choices in an effort to be more respectful, it pays to be sure they are all acceptable. Also, it is wise to avoid asking a young child if he wants to do something. For example, "Do you want to put on your coat?" will often get a no answer, even if he wishes to do it.

In stressing cooperation instead of obedience in our instructions to our children, we have respected the person and his wishes and feelings, so we get the cooperation we need. It may have taken a little longer, but still less time than dealing with a crying, unhappy child. Best of all, we are both more content.

Using "I" and "We" Messages

One of the best ways to get cooperation and avoid resistance is to give "I" or "we" messages. When we use them, the child feels respected. He is treated like a thinking human being instead of an automaton or robot. He can respond to our request and feel good about himself because he has some control over his actions.

Examples of "I" Messages

The phrases in italics are beginnings that can be used in many situations. Almost anything you consider misbehavior can be approached in this way.

> "*I need* you to stay right near me."
> "*I want* you to come home right after school."
> "*I worry when* you don't tell me where you're going."
> "*It bothers me when* you keep banging the basket."
> "*I don't like it when* you talk to me that way. Here's how I'd like you to say it." (Model words and tone you want.)

With the "I" message technique, the child does not feel scolded, just informed. If it is just that he did not know, we have taken care of the reason for the misbehavior. If we think it is a bid for more attention or empathy, we can give it. (Empathy is treated in the next chapter.) Most important, we have respected the child by trying to solve the problem rather than by scolding him.

Certain things we want our children to do apply to us parents, too, or to the whole family. The "we" message makes the request more acceptable because we are including ourselves or the family, not just the one child. My adult son says this was a powerful influence on him as a child. He wanted to do things as the family did them.

Examples of "We" Messages	Instead of
We always walk across the street.	Don't run.
We have to leave now.	Come on. Right now!
Let's hurry so we won't be late.	Hurry up! You'll make us late."

In the case of needing to correct a child, we can be very firm with "I" messages, but we will not get strong resistance because the child does not feel personally attacked. He understands that it is just his action that is being criticized. We have the most success in correcting a child when we are clear and respectful. The "I" and "we" messages accomplish both.

Considering the Child's Age and Development

A child's age and development, of course, have a big influence on what he can do. Knowing the various stages of child development through reading good books on the subject helps, but each child has his own pattern of maturing. As parents, we need to be in tune with our child and expect only what he is able to do. We need to back off a bit in our expectations if the child is not able to meet them.

Success in toilet training is related to developmental maturity. A young child needs to be interested, and his muscles need to be capable of cooperating. This usually happens between two and three years of age. I do not consider toilet training a matter of discipline, since the child has to be physiologically and psychologically ready for it. A natural interest develops in a child to use the potty and join older children in growing up when he is capable of doing so. I suggest having a potty available from the time a child is about two, then follow the child's lead. When he shows bladder control by staying dry for long periods, try the potty after meals and nap if the child is interested. When all indications point to readiness, switch to training pants (thick cotton underpants) during the day so the child begins to understand the change from diapers to potty. Be prepared for back sliding! For example, we moved to a different house in the middle of toilet training and had to start all over again. As hard as it is to develop, a relaxed attitude helps success come with the least amount of trauma to child and parent.

In considering maturity levels, it is important for us to keep certain "givens" in mind. Young children cannot put off their needs for food and rest. They often forget things, like bringing home their jackets or staying out of the mud. They cannot understand directions with too many steps or big words. We have better luck with simple one-or-two step instructions and easy-to-understand words. We can also give reminders to help the child do what is expected. Success is the goal. It is good for the self image of both children and parents. We are the ones who can make success possible by being sure the behavior is do-able.

Sometimes children want to do something beyond their maturity level. "Mommy, I'd rather do it myself," is not just a made-up phrase! For example, a young child may want to pour milk from the carton into his glass. We can say, "Here, let me help you," instead of "Don't pour your milk. You'll spill it." If he comes back with, "No, I want to do it," you can say, "The carton is too heavy for you. I can help," or, "We can put some in a little pitcher for you to pour." Both alternatives are acceptable. If he still resists, we can show empathy. "I know you wish you could pour the milk like your big sister. You'll be able to do it when you're bigger. For now, I need to help you."

All these actions show respect for the child, because it considers his stage of development. If we expect too much, we are setting up our child for unnecessary scoldings, put-downs and frustrations. If we expect only what the child is able to do, success and good feelings follow. On the other hand, if we expect too little, we are making him dependent.

Constantly changing maturity levels makes being a parent a continual challenge. We need to be sensitive to our children and be flexible in our expectations, adjusting up or down from day to day, week to week. This allows our children to grow at their own pace as smoothly as possible for both parent and child.

Accentuating The Positive

How many times have we had our children ask permission to do something and absent-mindedly answered, "No, not now?" This was likely followed by the child's pestering for a change in answer or just doing what he wanted anyway. Perhaps the next time, he did not even ask! On our part, often we did not follow through with prohibiting the action because it did not seem that important. "No" meant nothing.

Not only do children ignore us if we do not follow through, they rebel against too many no's. It makes them feel unloved and unapproved of, and they feel that their needs and wants are not being respected. We can expect lots of resistance.

When we find ourselves saying, "No" a lot, it is time to try something new. We can think through each of their requests carefully and answer, "Yes," to everything possible. Most of the things children want to do are all right. If the answer is, "No," we need a good reason, and we need to stick to it. For example. If a child wants to buy candy in the grocery store, we can say, "No, not this time. We have some candy at home."

"No" means something when we use it sparingly, have a good reason, and follow through. Children are not afraid to ask permission when the answer is usually, "Yes." In addition, they will accept the occasional no without putting up a fuss if they know we have carefully considered their request and have a good reason for our decision. My grown daughter said that my giving a valid reason for a no answer when she was a child made it much easier to accept.

Another way of getting children to be more willing to do what we ask is to say it in a positive way. We need to say *what we want, not what we do not want.* This allows them to cooperate with what we wish them to do instead of feeling that they have been doing something wrong.

Examples of Positive Statements

(It almost goes without saying that they need to be said in a respectful way, not barked out like orders.)

The Positive Statement	Instead of
Please stay close to me.	Don't run around.
Keep your voice down.	Don't talk so loud.
Touch with your eyes.	Don't touch.
Please sit down in the cart.	Don't stand up.
Here's a hankie.	Don't keep sniffling.
Couches are for sitting.	Don't jump on the couch.
Play with your toys on the floor.	Don't play on the table.

Of course, there are times to use the negative, especially in an emergency: "Don't touch. It's hot!" "Don't cross the street! A car's coming."

However, we need to be sure our reason is valid. "Don't run! You'll fall down," is tuned out because usually the child does not fall. "Don't run! You might fall," works better because it is believable.

Another example of using the positive is to distract a child who is doing something unacceptable. Once when I was responsible for a headstrong four-year-old (not my own) who was waving a toy sword around in a dangerous way, I suggested, "Let's put the sword in its sheath," and he did!

If that had not worked, I would have given an "I" message. "I can't let you do that. It's too dangerous. Where shall we put it?" This would have taken the blame off the child and let him cooperate without losing face. It may sound harder than saying, "Put that down," but the desired results are more likely.

Keeping Crystal Clear

Part of being respectful to another person is being clear in what we ask or say. None of us likes being blamed for something we did not understand in the first place. We have a special obligation to be crystal clear with children because they are not mind readers and they are not mature enough to handle overly complicated instructions or vocabularies. Also, children often have their own private logic.

In giving instructions to young children, it is important to keep vocabulary simple. Children are often slow to ask the meaning of a word they do not understand, nodding in agreement or listening with wide eyes, hoping that they can guess what we mean. Misunderstanding can be dangerous. It is always distressing and often leads to a scolding. We are on safe ground if we use words that we know our children understand, or when we do use a new word, that we add a phrase which explains the meaning. Especially after important instructions, we can say, "Do you have some questions?" Asking, "Do you understand what I mean?" can put children on the defensive. They often say, "Yes," even when they do not understand.

Many times children need reminders to remember even simple instructions given in familiar words. Giving whatever help is needed for success is a good investment, because success is the most powerful tool of all to build the child's self esteem. If a child wanders off, say, "I need you to stay right with me. Here, hold my hand," instead of, "Didn't I tell you to stay with me? How many times do I have to tell you?" This last makes a child feel defeated and resentful and does not work as well as making the child feel good about cooperating with instructions.

Another pitfall to overcome in giving clear instructions is some children's singularly private logic. There are often instructions in which we infer meanings. When I used to call one of my friends on the phone, her preschooler would sometimes answer. I would ask, "Is your mother home?" "Yes," he would say, then wait for the next question. I soon learned I had to be specific with, "May I speak to your mother?" He would then answer, "Yes, I'll get her." As another example of a child's private logic, one mother told me she ran into trouble correcting her child for misbehavior because she said, "Don't let me catch you eating a cookie before dinner." The child thought it was all right as long as he did not get caught!

Staying Open-Minded

When a child comes up with an idea about a situation, our first reaction is usually impatience. Often, however, the child has a really good idea, one we have not thought of. Instead of following the line of least resistance and saying, "Do it and quit arguing," we can say, "That's an interesting idea. Tell me why you think it'll be better that way." We show respect by being willing to listen.

Sometimes the idea is better, and in other cases it does not really matter if it is done his way. We make him feel included and worthwhile by considering his ideas and following his suggestion. If, on the other hand, we still believe our plan of action is best, the child will accept our decision if we state a good reason and he feels truly listened to. In this way, the parent is in charge, whether the child's or the parent's idea is followed.

Another benefit of listening to our children with an open mind is that we encourage them to have ideas and think through situations. This helps them develop problem-solving skills and self discipline—both worthy long-range goals for our children. Also, we are being models for them to be open-minded with others.

Being Non-Judgmental

Acting or talking in a judgmental way is one of the hardest things for us as parents to overcome. It is almost automatic to put our hands on our hips as we say, "Aren't you ever coming home on time?" Yet, we immediately set up a defensive situation in which our children argue, sulk or feel put down. If we can say, "How come you're late?" we might discover that he did not know the time or had to go back for his sweater; or we might get an innocent, "Am I late?" Then things can be worked out. Maybe the child needs a watch with an alarm, a reminder call to come home, or an understanding about why it is important that he get home on time. "I worry when you're late," or, "I want you home in time for dinner," can help him realize why being on time is important.

There are lots of ways, many of them subtle, in which we come across as judgmental—or laying blame—which make our children feel put down. Things to *avoid* are:

- **Being sarcastic in word or facial expression.** Say, "Time to put away your toys," instead of, "It's about time you put away your toys."

- **Name calling.** Say, "Time to wash your hands," instead of, "You're a mess. Wash your hands."

- **Judgmental body language.** Such things as hands on hips or shaking a finger.

- **Heaving a big sigh.**

- **Using the words "should" and "ought."** Say, "I want

you to stay by me," instead of, "You should stay by me," or, "You ought to know better than to get out of my sight."

- Patting a child on the head, chucking him under the chin, talking down to him as though he were much younger than he is, or speaking for a child when he can answer for himself all make him feel put down.

If we can retrain ourselves and consciously be non-judgmental in relating to our children, we can avoid lots of defensive and resistant actions and concentrate on working together and being cooperative. A non-judgmental approach keeps everyone feeling good about himself, and time and energy can go to solving problems instead of creating new ones.

Answering Questions In A Serious Way

Nothing is more distressing than asking a question in all seriousness and having people laugh or give a flip answer. Yet parents too often do this to children. It is the ultimate put-down or humiliation. Often children's questions seem silly or out-of-place because the answer is obvious to us, yet asking questions is the way a child learns. We not only hurt his feelings if we laugh or make a sarcastic remark, we discourage him from asking other questions. For example, a child might ask, "Does the saddle grow on the horse?" (A question I had as a child). The answer, "Of course not," makes him feel put down, whereas a simple explanation of how the horse is saddled for riding helps the child learn.

A good guideline is to treat the question with as much seriousness as it is asked. If we can avoid judgmental replies such as, "Of course," "What a silly question," or, "Don't be ridiculous," and instead give straightforward answers, we encourage the child to keep asking what he thinks are good questions and continue learning about the world around him.

Respecting A Child's Space

Getting along with children, as well as people of all ages, involves respecting their "space." I mean belongings and physical space, such as a child's toys and room, even his side of the room, as well as the things we cannot see or touch, such as privileges, responsibilities and ideas. All of these things are tied up with the child's self image and feeling of worth, and he will resist anyone's challenging them. This is especially true with young children who are struggling to establish themselves and again with teenagers who are making the supreme and often rocky effort to break away from parents and become adults. Respect for space is respect for the person.

Many squabbles between children are over toys or other belongings. To insist that a young child "share" is a hopeless task. To him, sharing means giving up something he wants or that belongs to him, neither of which he does willingly. However, if we protect that child's belongings and help him feel in control, he will eventually "share" of his own accord. For example, if Aaron is playing with a toy that is his and a second child asks for it, we can say, "Zachary wants to play with your toy. Can he have a turn with it?" If Aaron says, "Yes," everyone is happy. If he says, "No," we can explain to Zachary that the toy belongs to Aaron and offer Zachary another toy to play with. In a few days, or even the same day, Aaron will willingly give someone else a turn with his toy because we have helped establish that it is his and under his control. In another scenario, if Zachary grabs the toy from Aaron, we can take the toy, give it back to Aaron and say, "That toy belongs to Aaron. We'll have to ask him if you can play with it." We not only protect Aaron's belongings or "space," but help Zachary learn respect for other people's property. This scenario actually happened with my son when he was about 18 months old.

Respecting A Child's Space

Many resentments between brothers and sisters, no matter what age, can be avoided if we very carefully develop the idea of respect for each other's property—not only toys, but clothes, books, paper, or anything the child has. When children are young and very close in age, it can help greatly to give specific toys to each child and not have many toys jointly owned. If toys belong to more than one sibling, the older will usually control the play period, and the younger ones build up resentment. On the other hand, if parents overprotect the younger children, resentment is created in the older child. Major equipment, such as a swing set or sand box, is obviously a family belonging with which several can play at once, but toy trucks and dolls, for example, are crisis-makers for young children unless they each have their own. Even blocks can be a problem for children who are too young to play cooperatively. This can be handled by giving some floor space and blocks to each child, being sure that each one keeps control over his own portion.

As children get older, they are more and more concerned about their physical space—their room, dresser, desk. It's very important to them that their things are not moved, taken, or borrowed without permission, and they especially resent their dressers being rummaged through.

Now comes the matter of keeping the room up to family standards. We need to set standards for neatness, but our children will be more cooperative if they can make some decisions about where things go. We as parents might have a standard that before bedtime each night everything must be picked up from the floor and put in storage that is provided, but the child could have some say in how his toys are organized. The child who has a hard time being neat might do better with covered boxes or drawers, rather than shelves.

If a young child has a hard time picking up his things by himself, we can offer help. For example, we can say, "Let's pick up your room. Where shall we put this?" If he resists, we can sidestep the issue by saying, "When we've picked up your room, we'll have lunch," or, "We'll read a story if there is time after your room is picked up."

Another example of space is a child's creative work, such as a special block structure. If he does not want to tear it down when it comes time to put away his toys, we can let him leave it up if at all possible. If there is a younger brother or sister who might knock over the treasured work, we can save a lot of conflict by putting a gate across the door to protect the block creation.

Now we get into intangible examples of "space"— things we cannot see or touch, like privileges, responsibilities and ideas. Teenage children are especially sensitive to lack of respect for these areas. If we can get in the habit of respecting our young children's space, this respect will grow with the children as they get older and not be such a problem.

An example of a privilege might be a child's sitting in a certain chair at dinner. If this is changed suddenly without asking permission and giving an explanation, we can expect resentment. However, if we say, "Can the baby sit in your place now that she can eat with us at the table? I need to help her with her meals." Instead of feeling displaced, the older child feels respected, and cooperation will follow.

Children like having responsibilities they are mature enough to handle. The amazing thing is that they can even resent someone's doing their job for them without permission. It is their space, and they do not like anyone intruding. Instead of just doing it, we can say, "Can I set the table for you tonight?" If we get permission to enter his space, there is no problem.

A teenager's space is more tricky because there are so many dynamics at work. What to wear to school can sometimes be a source of friction. He might want to wear clothes which we feel inappropriate. We can ask, "Why is this so important to you?" He might explain that it's the style, it's more comfortable, and it is not against the school rules. Even though we prefer another mode of dress, if it is not harmful, against the school dress code, or we do not feel strongly about it, there is not a good reason to deny the privilege. We have listened to our teenager, respected his point of view, and agreed to what he wants since we did not have valid reasons to refuse.

On the other hand, if our teenager wants to wear short cutoffs or holey jeans because "everyone is wearing them" and we have strong convictions against the choice, we can refuse permission to wear such clothes. We might say, "I believe that such clothing doesn't show respect for the teachers or school and doesn't create a learning atmosphere. Learning is important. That's your job right now." Even if the teenager has a tattered pair of jeans he changes into at school, he will still know where we stand, and these values will stick with him.

Ideas are the hardest kind of space with which to deal. If we are open-minded, non-judgmental and good listeners, we can evaluate a new idea together with our children and see if it fits into the general family values. With this practice, children do not need to be on the defensive, and arguments can often be avoided. Respect for budding ideas, even if we disagree, encourages creative thinking. It's important how we respond to teenager's ideas, since they are making that essential break from being a dependent child to adulthood. However, they are suspended between two realms for a while, vacillating back and forth. They have new ideas but still need our guidance. To give that guidance respectfully and not cause resentment is a real challenge.

Following is an example of interacting with a teenager on the touchy issue of the legal drinking age. He might say, "I think it should be legal to drink at 18, since we can be drafted into military service and risk our lives in war." Perhaps you are very much against lowering the age, but instead of responding with, "That's a crazy idea. We'd have more drunk teenagers than ever," you could say, "You have a good point, but there are still some things that worry me. I think that even more teenagers would drink too much, as well as drive under the influence."

Even though you disagree, you have respected his ideas while giving yours. It may even come about, as you get into the discussion, that you will get a new insight into the issue. Parents can get new ideas from teenagers, as well as give them. Of prime importance is that we have not put the teenager on the defensive. It gives the teenager a chance to mull over our ideas and add them to his own thinking. If our ideas are logical and not forced on him, he will fit them into his own value system. We need to be patient, however, because mulling over ideas takes time.

Insisting on Respect For Parents' Space, Too

We have talked a lot about respecting a child's space. I think it is important, too, that we parents insist on respect for our space from our children, whether they be young, teenage or somewhere in between.

The most common form of disrespect for our space is a child's talking back or being sassy. It is best to nip back-talk in the bud, but it needs to be stopped even if it has gotten a head start. "I" messages avoid resentment and still get the message across. We can say firmly, "I don't like it when you talk to me like that. If you disagree, say it respectfully."

It is important to model just how we want our children to talk because children—the young ones at least—might not understand what we mean by "respectfully." We can explain, "I'd rather you say it like this: I don't want to wear this sweater because it's too hot." In your example include not only the words but the tone of voice wanted. It is best not to ask for an apology or for the child to repeat the phrase with the tone of voice wanted at the time. It will cause resentment, because the child feels embarrassed. We have informed him, and that is all that is needed. He can do it the way we want next time, and he will be much more willing to do so if he has not been humiliated.

Parents' belongings, physical space, ideas, and privileges, such as sitting in a special chair in the living room or at the table, need to be respected too—just like the child's. The ideal is mutual respect.

Respect for space is one of the hardest forms of respect to develop, but it has a big payoff. When we think about relationships between parents and children, brothers and sisters, adult family members, bosses and workers, we will see that most problems and resentments are caused by one person's entering another's space. Once we are sensitive to this, we can develop the habit of asking ourselves, "Am I entering someone else's space?" before we speak or act. If we avoid such an invasion, things will go smoother for all concerned.

Everything we do with our children is teaching them behavior for the future. By treating our children with genuine respect and insisting that we are treated the same way, we are teaching them to have respect for others and for themselves, a powerful asset.

3

EMPATHY

Empathy, the third necessary element in preventive discipline, is a seldom used concept and one often misunderstood. By empathy I mean showing an understanding of how another person feels—something most effective when expressed in words to that person.

Empathy for a Broken Doll

Empathy is often confused with sympathy, but there is an important difference. Sympathy gives the message that we feel sorrow or pity for the person. It is often rejected because it can imply that we think the person is weak or in a hopeless situation. Empathy, on the other hand, shows understanding and is non-judgmental. It simply acknowledges how the person feels.

For example, if a family has to move and experiences a serious lowering in standard of living, a child might act out if she now has to share a room with a sibling. We can show empathy by saying, "I'll bet you wish we were back in our old house where you had your own room." Such a comment would make her feel understood and help her not feel so resentful. However, if we make a sympathetic statement instead, like, "Poor Sally, you used to have a room of your own, and now you have to share with your little sister," we reinforce her resentment. Even though the statement is true, we have not dealt with her feelings at all.

Quite often children are faced with situations that are hard or impossible to change, as in the above example. The most common are:

- a new baby in the family,
- the child's not getting or doing something wished for,
- feeling discriminated against,
- moving to a new area,
- parents' divorce or the death of someone close.

Empathy can be our best help in such cases. We cannot change how a child feels by pointing out all the reasons she should not feel that way. She will either spend an enormous amount of energy trying to convince us of how she does feel or just repress the feelings altogether. Either way, no progress is made. When we let the child know we understand her feelings, she can move beyond those feelings toward solutions.

Since children are not mind-readers, we need to say what we understand in words, and it is important what words we use. "I understand how you feel," is not effective because the child has no way of knowing what we "understand." She will probably say or think, "No, you don't understand." A better way is to make a statement of how we think she feels. For example, if a child is acting distressed after a special friend has moved away, we can say, "You must be very lonely without Cynthia." Then she can agree, add something more specific, or even be non-committal. We may or may not get at exactly what is bothering her, but at least she knows we are trying to understand.

A New Baby In The Family

We have all heard a new baby called "a bundle of joy." However, it is anything but that to the child who has to make the supreme adjustment of sharing her parents' time and giving up the limelight of being the baby or only child in the family. She sometimes even verbalizes her feelings with, "When can we take it back?" or acts out by pinching the baby.

Besides giving the child the best attention possible, even though we are exhausted, we can acknowledge her feelings by saying, "I'll bet you wish Mommy wasn't so busy with the new baby." She probably *is* finding it hard, and such a statement makes her feel understood, helping melt away resentment. It can also encourage her to say how she feels and to ask some questions. This provides a good opening for suggesting ways she can be involved in this new adventure. We could ask her to get a diaper or a toy for the baby, or we might suggest that she hum or sing a tune to entertain the baby. She probably is not ready to be called "a big girl" yet, because she wishes she were a baby again. It is best to stick to suggestions of ways she can stay in the picture.

The Child's Not Getting Or Doing Something Wished For

Children often want to do or have something that we believe is impossible, at least at the moment. Usually a child will accept a good reason for a "no" answer, if explained in an honest, respectful way. But there are times when nothing can convince her to accept no without a struggle. That is where empathy comes in. For example, if a child wants an ice cream cone but you cannot stop to get one, the first step is to give a logical reason why the answer is no. If you get strong resistance, you can say, "I know you'd really like an ice cream cone." Then, "We can't stop now because we have to get home right away, but there's some there you can have after lunch," or, "We'll get some next time we go to the grocery store." Showing understanding plus hope for the future makes the child feel that you are with her instead of against her, and resistance is much less.

The following area is where I had the most personal experience with empathy, and I considered it an invaluable helper. When my son was a toddler, he often did not want to leave the playground to go home. Depending on the situation, I would say something like, "I know you really like to play in that sandbox, and you want to stay longer." Then, "I wish you could stay, but we have to go home now and fix dinner. We can come back another day" (if really possible). Then I would distract him with some toy or comment, and we would get by without tears or a struggle.

In another example, my twin daughters sometimes wanted a toy I did not want to buy. If I got strong resistance I would say, "I know you'd like to have that toy." Then, "We can't get it today, but maybe you could put it on your birthday wish list" (or some other realistic statement). That worked fine, and it gave us ideas for birthdays.

In an experience with a child outside my family, empathy broke a stalemate. A friend with an eight-year-old son and I were delivering some Christmas presents from our church to a family we had "adopted" for the holiday season. There were quite a few things to carry, so when my friend opened the trunk of her car she said to her son, "Carry some of the packages for us." He just stood there staring at the contents of the trunk. His mother tried again to get him to help, but to no avail. Remembering what I had learned about empathy with my own children, I said, "I bet you wish the presents were for you." Then, "It will be Christmas before long, and you'll have presents under your tree. These are for the family that the church adopted." He then took an armload of presents and carried them to the family's apartment. I had resisted the temptation to be judgmental and just stated how I thought he felt and the facts of the situation. I was grateful that empathy had changed balkiness into willingness. It was like magic.

Many temper tantrums can be avoided by showing empathy. It takes away that utter frustration a child feels when she is denied something she wants very much. Although the answer is still no, it includes understanding and hope for the future. (A section on temper tantrums appears in a later part of the book.)

Feeling Discriminated Against

Children sometimes feel they are being discriminated against, and it makes them extremely frustrated. It may be that an older brother or sister has more privileges and there is no way she can catch up to them in age. We can empathize by saying, "I bet you wish you could stay up as late as Peggy." Then, "She's older than you and doesn't need as much sleep. When you are older you can stay up later, too."

If a child feels that an older sibling is getting too many privileges, it can be a signal for parents to think through what that younger child is allowed to do. It may be that she is old enough to have her privileges extended a little. It can also be a signal to consider whether we are showing favoritism for one child over another by letting one have certain privileges that the other deserves, too.

These are things we can adjust. Evaluation of the reactions of our children to limits and conditions we expect, and a possible adjustment in them, is not a sign of giving in to demands. It is a necessary part of being good parents.

Moving To A New Area

Few families these days stay in one place for the lifetime of their children. There are many reasons to move— a job change, moving up in standard of living, or moving down. No matter what the reason, good or bad, it is usually hard for children to move, unless they are very young, when their lives center completely around the immediate family. The minute they learn to play cooperatively, a move involves many losses, because it means a change in friends, activities and routines.

Our family had a difficult experience with moving when my son was five. He left behind many good friends he was looking forward to having as kindergarten classmates. We found that he acted out in little, mischievous ways. For example, I was visited by the local minister and attempted to include my five-year-old in the conversation. However, before long my son asked in a loud, clear voice, "When is he going to leave?"

Looking back, I think that more empathy would have helped my son's adjustment and, consequently, made it much easier for the rest of the family. I wish I had said, "You must miss your old friends; I bet you wish we'd never moved." What I did was concentrate on activities in which he could make new friends. That was helpful, but I think some good empathy could have made the period of adjustment much shorter and smoother for all of us. Empathy would have shown that we understood his feelings and helped him in his efforts to get beyond them.

Parents' Divorce Or The Death Of Someone Close

Except for the death of a parent, a divorce is often the most traumatic event with which a child has to deal. Divorce can mean loss of the love and care of one of the parents and the beginning of a very different way of life. Very often, divorce leads to a serious drop in standard of living. All this can be very disturbing to the child and can lead to acting out or withdrawal. There are lots of dynamics at work—a change of life style, perhaps a feeling of guilt, and plain loneliness for the missing parent. You can say, "You must miss Daddy a lot. I know it's hard for you, and I'm sorry it has to be this way." This can open the door for the child to say how she feels and ask questions that bother her.

I have not had personal experience with divorce so cannot draw on actual events. I have had experience, however, with the power of empathy. A close friend of mine was quite depressed for several months because a job she had did not work out. Many close friends tried to cheer her up by attempting to talk her out of her depression or taking her to lunch, but to no avail. Suddenly, the weight of the world seemed lifted off her shoulders and she began to act like her old, buoyant self again. When asked what had accomplished this miracle, she replied that a psychologist friend had said to her, "You must have been very disappointed that the job didn't work out for you." That one statement of empathy by the psychologist did what all the good intentions of friends could not accomplish.

Empathy can also be very helpful when a child experiences the death of someone close. When my father died a few years ago, many of the family members gathered at the old homestead in Oregon after the funeral. Since a number of us were from too far away to go home for the night, we slept in beds and on couches all over the house. I happened to sleep next to my nine-year-old niece, who had spent a lot of time with her grandfather and was very close to him. She got quite sick to her stomach in the night and was thoroughly miserable. I helped her through her ordeal, and then we sat on the couch and talked. Having a hunch that her distress over her grandfather's death had a great deal to do with her getting sick, I said, "You must miss Granddad a lot." After a pause, she answered, "Yeah, but I'm sure glad he had his glasses on, because now he can read." In his casket at the funeral, my father's glasses were in place. My niece and I talked quite a while, and finally she got sleepy and went back to her bed. Empathy had opened doors and certainly helped us both in that sad time.

The same approach is helpful when a child experiences any big change. Empathy can help avoid more serious psychological consequences, because reactions are dealt with as they occur. However, there are times when an empathetic parent may not be enough. In that case, there are a number of books with helpful advice on how to deal with serious problems, and it is in the best interests of everyone concerned to get all the information we can. In addition, the good, empathetic parent must be alert to the need for professional help when advisable.

To summarize, empathy helps a child, or an adult for that matter, get beyond her feelings of resistance and frustration over things beyond her control by our acknowledging those feelings in words. It is best done with a statement suggesting what we *think* the person is feeling, rather than saying only, "I *know* how you feel," or asking what she feels. She usually cannot or will not answer. Making an exploratory statement and then pausing for a reaction gives her a chance to agree, come up with feelings we did not pinpoint, or remain noncommittal. Most important, the child feels understood and supported. That is a powerful step in moving from debilitating feelings to solutions. It is an important stepping stone in effective preventive discipline in that it can avoid unproductive behavior.

PART TWO
PATHS THAT HELP AVOID MISBEHAVIOR

4

SETTING LIMITS

One does well to remember that the familiar "an ounce of prevention is worth a pound of cure" is especially true in disciplining children. Setting limits is a very important part of any preventive discipline, for it helps the child know what is expected and thereby avoids a great deal of misbehavior. For purposes of exploring the ideas in this book, I define misbehavior as a child's inappropriate action in any given situation—in other words, a child's doing just what we do not want him to do. There are five steps that help set limits successfully. They are:

1. Set limits *before* an event.

2. Make limits clear and reasonable.

3. Give directions or limits in the positive, whenever possible.

4. Be consistent and follow through.

5. Set logical consequences if limits are not followed.

You will recognize elements of both respect and empathy as each step is explained and examples given.

Setting Limits Before The Event

Setting limits before the child is in the situation lets him know what you expect and goes a long way toward avoiding his doing the wrong thing. Most children want to please if they know what to do and do not have to lose face doing it.

It is very useful to have a general philosophy about your limits. Here are the guidelines that work for me: any behavior by the child is all right if 1) it is safe, 2) is not harmful to health, and 3) is socially acceptable. (This includes fitting into family schedules and values.) These guidelines made it easy for me to decide on limits and to be able to remember them, an important factor in being consistent.

It is important to think through each situation and not "let old tapes play"—that is, be limited by the attitudes that we learned from our parents. We can all too easily set the same limits our parents set, even if we thought they were terrible when we were children! It is best to think about each situation with an open mind and decide the limits anew, ourselves.

Here are some "limits" examples for use in anticipation of an event. They are designed for young children, but the principles work for older children, as well.

Before a birthday party, you might say, "The party is for Jimmy, so he will open all his presents. Also, when you are eating cake and ice cream, stay sitting down so food doesn't get all over. We don't want to make things hard for Jimmy's mother." (Socially acceptable.)

When arriving at the zoo, you could suggest: "Stay near me so we don't get lost from each other. We don't feed or tease the animals because it isn't good for them. Just look and enjoy." There are times, however, when a negative statement is necessary: "Don't put your hand on the cage" is one example, but here the tone of voice makes a big difference in how it comes across. (Safety of the child.)

In leaving for a friend's house on a cold day, you could say: "I want you to wear your jacket so you won't get chilled and catch cold." (Health.)

If going to a wedding you might say: "You'll need to be very quiet and stay sitting by me. This is a very special day for Dave and June, and we need to watch quietly." (Socially acceptable.)

Everything has a logical reason, so it is easy to remember. Giving a reason also teaches self discipline for future events.

Making Limits Reasonable And Clear

We need to think about the maturity of the child in setting reasonable limits. A young toddler cannot remember to stay close. He needs to be in a shopping cart, holding our hand or attached to us by a wrist bracelet. If you want him in the shopping cart and he does not want to be there, an "I" message is in order. You can say, "I need you to sit in the cart while I shop. That's your job." For me, it worked well when my children were cart-riding age to let them snack on a box of crackers that was part of my shopping.

When my children got older and were accompanying me on foot, I set limits of being relatively quiet, staying in the same aisle with me, and keeping their hands off the merchandise unless they had permission to pick up something. They nearly always got some treat as a reward for a good shopping trip. Of their own accord, they did not expect a treat when they were past kindergarten age, so it did not set a precedent in our family.

Limits need to be fair and reasonable. The situation makes a difference. Most children can adjust to grocery shopping when we keep on the move, but few can tolerate our shopping for a dress or a coat when we have to try them on and make hard decisions. My four-year-old son was no problem when we went grocery shopping, so I decided to take him with me when I was looking for a new dress. He soon got bored and began running through the racks of dresses—not between the racks, but *between the dresses on the racks.* Of course, I was terribly embarrassed. When I finally caught him, I remember squeezing his arm hard and saying to him through clenched teeth, "We're going home!" That is probably just what he wanted. Upon reflection, I realized that I was expecting too much of him at his age. I never took him on such a shopping trip again.

If we are going visiting or expect a long wait in the doctor's office, children can follow the limits we have set—for example, being quiet and not running around— if we have a few toys and books along. In other words, we can help them be successful. Children are essentially reasonable and will do what we suggest if it is fair and within their maturity level.

Individual differences count, too. Some young children can sit quietly in church or through an adult program, while others cannot. My preschool son was one who could not sit still in church, while one of my friends had a daughter who sat as quietly as any adult. I had to take my son out during the service because he was so wiggly. Later an elderly neighbor asked him why I took him out of church. He replied, "Because I wasn't being cooperative." He knew that word well. I decided it was best to make other arrangements for him during church and other adult gatherings that took long, quiet sitting.

Giving Directions Or Limits In The Positive

Expressing ourselves in the positive can save a lot of time and effort on our part, and resistance on the child's part. Children do not like to be told that they *cannot* do something. They are much more interested in what they *can* do. For example, when you are going as a family to a restaurant for dinner, you can say, "At the restaurant we are guests, so we keep our voices down and stay in our chairs." It is amazing how well even young children can respond to such positive preparation.

Being Consistent And Following Through

Children can be very persistent. They sometimes keep after us to do or get whatever they want, even after we have said "No" and given a good reason. All is lost unless we follow through, to be sure the limit is followed. We also need to be consistent in expecting that the limit be met every time the situation comes up, unless there is some special circumstance. I remember overhearing a conversation my five-year-old son was having with a friend that made me glad I had learned the lesson of consistency and follow-through. "Ask your mom if you can come over to my house," said the friend. My son replied, "I already did, and she said, 'No,' because it's too close to dinner." "Ask again, she might change her mind," urged the friend. It was music to my ears to hear my son say, "It won't do any good. When she says no, she means no."

If we have thought through the limit and believe it is truly fair and reasonable, we will not have trouble sticking to it. I might add, however, that if a child protests strongly, it may be time to think through the limit again and consider whether the child has matured since that particular one was set. Maybe it is time to relax the limits a bit.

Special Circumstances

Unusual situations might call for different limits. For example, a special get-together or TV program could be a reason for a later bedtime. Once when my son was a young teenager, he wanted to watch a special late movie on TV. (In those years TV only had movies from 11 PM to 1 AM, and there were no VCRs or videos.) I said "No" to the late movie because it was a school night and I thought he needed the sleep. He argued and fussed because it would be his only chance to see this movie. Well, the upshot was that we argued until way past his bedtime, and both of us were exhausted and unhappy. After that I gave permission for extra-special TV programs. In fact, we watched the classic movie *The Grapes of Wrath* together a few months later at the late 11-1 hour. Now with VCRs, there would not be a problem, but I think the principle of giving occasional permission for a change in limits is a good and reasonable one.

Setting Logical Consequences If Limits Are Not Followed

No matter how hard we try to set limits in a good way, sometimes they are not followed. We need to problem-solve and figure out why. Maybe the limits were too difficult or beyond the maturity level of the child. Maybe he did not understand or he forgot. Maybe there is some other good reason. Maybe he is resentful about something—such as not getting his share of attention, thinking a sibling is getting more privileges, or believing that something else is not fair. If we can get at the reason for not following the limits, we can usually make adjustments to change the situation.

Punishment, such as loss of unrelated privileges, grounding or not watching TV, is often unproductive, in my opinion. In fact it can be counterproductive, causing more resentment and resistance to limits. I have seen friends of my children be most resentful of such punishment. Getting to the bottom of the problem, making necessary adjustments when possible, and saying, "Next time I want you to. . .," is usually sufficient.

If this does not work, logical consequences, or a related loss of privilege, is the next step. For example, if he is late for dinner, let the meal get cold and do not wait on him when he does arrive. In other examples, if he runs around in a store, hold his hand all the time; or if he keeps tracking mud in the house, have him leave his shoes outside the door. An example of a logical consequence in my own family was that when any of my children forgot to take their lunch to school, I did not take it to them. I figured it was the logical consequence of not being responsible for something I thought they were old enough to take care of. To my way of thinking, missing one lunch would not hurt their health, and the inconvenience of not having a lunch, needing to borrow money to buy one, or sharing someone's sandwich would help them remember next time. It worked. They very seldom forgot their lunches.

If the consequences are logical, the child will learn limits and responsibilities better because cause and effect are related. Also the consequences are easier for parents to live with. An example of a consequence that is often harder on parent than child is "no TV for a week." Consequences that cannot be carried out do no good, either. I once heard a mother in the grocery store say, "Quit that or I'll call the police!"

Empathy can be another help in handling children's overstepping their limits. They may be jumping on the couch, even though they know they are supposed to keep their feet off the furniture. You can say, "Couches are for sitting. I know it's fun to jump on the couch, but it's bad for the couch. Let's find some place where you can jump."

Setting workable limits takes a good bit of thought and consideration to make them fair and logical, and it takes an additional effort to be consistent and follow through in applying them. However, it is well worth the effort when the result is well-behaved children.

5

EVERYDAY MISBEHAVIOR: SOME CAUSES AND WHAT TO DO

Misbehavior happens no matter how hard we may try to follow the idea of preventive discipline. I believe there is a cause for misbehavior. The child is responding, either consciously or subconsciously, to something beyond his control. He is acting out or withdrawing to try to gain control over the situation.

We need to problem-solve to try to figure out the reason for the misbehavior so we can deal with it. There follows a checklist to help pinpoint conditions that could lead to misbehavior or may account for any misbehavior that we are experiencing with our children. If we can figure out the reason, we can make the necessary adjustments or give empathy for things that cannot be changed.

Checklist of Possible Causes Of Misbehavior

1. First thing to consider: is she just tired, hungry or not well?

2. Is she bored?

3. Does she feel put down or humiliated?

4. Is she frustrated that she cannot work something, like a toy?

5. Does she feel unfairly treated in connection with siblings, responsibilities or other things?

6. Is she getting enough positive attention so that she feels loved, approved of, and has a sense of belonging? (We may be giving a lot, but to the child it is not enough.)

7. Is she too immature to do what we expect? Does she understand? Has she forgotten?

8. Is she jealous about a new baby or upset about a family death or divorce?

9. Has she not been given something she wants, even though we think she does not *need* it?

Making adjustments to correct the first five situations on the check list are fairly obvious—be sure the child gets food, rest and health care when needed; keep a child interested with activities, objects or conversation to keep her from getting bored; avoid humiliating a child in conversation or when correcting her; and help avoid frustration by either helping a child or putting the object away until she is older. If a child feels she is being treated unfairly, we can reevaluate and make adjustments when possible or give empathy when we cannot or do not think it wise to change the situation. The rest of the list is dealt with in more detail later in this chapter.

As an aside here, I should like to point out that some parents consider sex play as misbehavior. I think of it as natural curiosity, but I also believe it is best to steer children into other activities. This takes both supervision and the effort to provide a stimulating and challenging environment. It is best not to give the impression that you consider sex play "bad," since it might have a carry-over effect into the child's perception of her sexuality, especially later on. Instead, it can be an opening for talking with your child about whatever questions she may have at that moment concerning sex.

Lack Of Enough Positive Attention

Although any one of the factors in the above check list can lead to misbehavior, one of the most common causes, besides hunger and fatigue, is lack of the attention that a child needs. If a child does not get attention for the positive things she does, she is forced to misbehave to get it. As Harold Simpson, Project Psychologist for the San Bruno Head Start Program, once said, "Children are decision-makers, and they will make decisions come hell or high water." They will do whatever necessary to get the attention they crave. As mentioned in the chapter on attention, I did an observation as an adult for a college psychology class. The assignment was to observe the interaction of children with their care givers in a variety of situations and to write down what was said and done. What I saw was that when children were ignored, they invariably misbehaved until they got attention, even negative attention, such as a sharp reprimand. When they got good, positive attention, they were well-behaved.

Expecting Too Much Of The Child

Another common cause of misbehavior is expecting too much of the child. If children are expected to take on responsibilities that are beyond their maturity level or are too demanding of their energy or psychological strength, they will rebel as a matter of self preservation. For example, if a first grader is expected to get herself up and dressed, fix her lunch, and get off to school without prompts and helps, she may find it too heavy a responsibility. She may still need her mother's or father's support as she develops independence. I might add that even though the modern father takes on much more of the nurturing than formerly, children may insist that their mothers do certain parenting tasks.

As an example of a situation's being beyond the maturity level of a child, when our son was eight years old he became hard to live with, manifesting misbehavior that was bothersome, but not serious. We tried to problem-solve. After ticking off the things we were expecting of him, we realized that it was just too much for an eight-year-old. We backed off a bit, and life was smoother again. We were expecting too much of our older child; his twin sisters were four years old at the time.

Situations That Cannot Be Changed

Another important cause of misbehavior is a situation that is distressing to the child, but one that cannot be changed. Examples of this are a new baby in the family, a move to a different neighborhood, or a family loss brought on by death or divorce. Special efforts to minimize the effects can help, but ultimately the child has to adjust. As we see in the empathy chapter, well placed empathy helps the child accept the new situation because she at least feels understood. Also noted in that chapter, though, is the fact that professional help is sometimes needed to meet these more serious problems.

The Spoiled Child—Needs Versus Wants

Misbehavior can also be evidence of (heaven forbid) a spoiled child. Sometimes without realizing it, we give a child too many wants instead of sticking mainly to needs. Meeting all a child's needs will not spoil the child; meeting all a child's wants will. How does one tell the difference?

Needs are necessary for normal development. The physical needs are basically for food, shelter, rest and good medical care. The psychological needs are mainly for love, approval and belonging. On the whole, a normal child will only demand as much as she needs. Sometimes it is more than the *parent* thinks the child needs, but if she needs it, she will try to get it.

As stated before, I believe that fulfilling a child's needs does not spoil the child. I further believe that it does not spoil a child to let her have or do *some* of things that she wants. It shows we value her and her ideas. However, giving her everything or nearly everything she asks for *will* spoil her. For example, if a child asks for and gets a toy every time she goes shopping, it becomes an expectation. A new toy so often is not a need; it is a want. Children need to play, but toys can be simple, such as boxes or blocks, and they can be multiuse, making it unnecessary to have new toys all the time for satisfying play.

A note of warning: if a child keeps wanting new toys, clothes, or treats, it could be a bid for attention. If she is not getting as much attention as she needs, she may ask for things to prove to herself that she is loved. Emotionally deprived children often want lots of *things*.

If a child wants a candy bar every time you go grocery shopping, it is a want, not a need. Candy does not constitute necessary food for development. An occasional candy bar will not spoil the child, but getting one too often could result in her expecting one every time. This leads to unnecessary expense, poor health habits, and an argument if you decide to say "No" at some point.

Another example of wants versus needs is clothes for children as they get older. Young children seldom care what they wear, but as they get into school, even preschool, they begin to want to dress like their peers. A certain amount of this fulfills a need to fit in, to belong. However, it can be carried to extremes and be very costly. One way to handle this is by a clothing allowance, with the child choosing which clothes to buy. For the older child, any additional clothes can be paid for by saving her allowance or earning her own money.

In each case, a certain amount of what a child wants is to fulfill a need, but at some point it becomes a pure want. That is where parental judgment comes in. We certainly wish to meet our children's needs, but catering to all their wants will lead to a spoiled child and to misbehavior if that want is not fulfilled.

The important thing to consider if a child misbehaves is that we need to pinpoint the reason and then do what we can about it. Even though it may take some time, thought and possibly outside help, adjustments can be made and life will be smoother once again.

6

EATING AND SLEEPING PROBLEMS

Eating and sleeping are two physical needs that have to be satisfied each day, yet parents and children often have different perceptions of what is required to satisfy them. Sometimes a battle of wills develops over the quantity and choice of food, and over bedtime. Since this is a daily interaction, children will often use this *battle* as a means to control their parents. This is a test for preventive discipline, since it requires attention, respect and empathy to arrive at a satisfactory routine for eating and for bedtime. Otherwise, children may learn how to "push their parents' buttons" by devious and teasing behavior. For example, they may insist that the parent cajole or plead with them to take each bite, or they may play with their food or make a mess of the meal on their plate. At bedtime, they may keep asking for drinks and stories, or cry pitifully.

It helps to realize that two things you cannot make a child do are eat and sleep. You can only make them come to the table and go to bed. Most child specialists believe that children will get enough food and sleep if they have some choice in the matter. This is not to say that children should be allowed to do whatever they want, but that we need to provide conditions for eating and sleeping that take into consideration their individual needs.

Happy Mealtimes

Here are some ideas for establishing good eating habits. Set the stage for a good appetite by limiting snacks and sweets between meals. A cookie, cracker or fruit in mid-morning or mid-afternoon will not spoil the child's appetite, but serious snacking will. Ideally, meals are eaten together as a family, but often a young child cannot wait so has to eat earlier. You can, however, have the same routine for meals whether eaten with the family or before.

One problem—and sometimes a big one—connected with eating is the difference in perception between parent and child of the quantity of food he needs. Some children are big eaters, while others have a metabolism that enables them to thrive on very little. The best test of whether they are getting enough is how their health and energy measure up. Your child's pediatrician can help evaluate this. Try putting the amount of food on the child's plate that he seems comfortable with so that he can finish it. He will let you know if it is not enough. Also, put the total array of food for that course on the plate so he can have a variety of tastes and the plate will look more like what the other family members have. Eating is a social event.

Good eating habits will develop if there are a few simple rules about meals, such as eating some of everything on the plate, trying at least one bite of a new food, not leaving the table during the meal except under special circumstances, and not having dessert unless an agreed upon minimum is eaten. Of course, this last condition assumes that the portions are realistic in size. (I consider dessert a reward, not a bribe.)

To keep dessert from becoming an issue, mention it once and then calmly enforce the no dessert edict if the conditions are not met. Do not let the child bargain by saying, for example, "If I eat all my beans, can I have dessert?" Establish in advance what is satisfactory and restate if the conditions are questioned. You have to be the judge as to whether the conditions have been met. If the child complains about a negative decision, point out that there will be another chance for dessert at the next meal. This method used to work quite well with our three children. However, when I used to say to our twins, "No dessert unless you eat your dinner," they would ask, "What's for dessert?" It inspired me to have interesting desserts, but the choice was still theirs!

New foods are often a problem. Tastes have to be cultivated. The rule that the child try at least one bite of a new food helps him get used to it. If he does not like it at all, wait a while to reintroduce it. And recognize that he simply may not like some foods; most of us dislike something. Multiple vitamins can be reassuring in providing the vitamins needed daily if the child will not eat certain essential foods. Also, it is good to remember that children have more sensitive taste buds than adults, so spicy or sharp tastes may be especially hard to accept. We need to avoid expecting our children to eat foods that are offensive to them.

It is well worth putting a lot of thought into productive mealtimes so that a daily battle is avoided. Mealtime is ideally a time to replenish our physical need for food and to have the good fellowship that feeds our psychological needs, as well.

"Now I Lay Me Down to Sleep"

A successful bedtime involves several things. The time has to be realistic for the child's need for sleep, and the bedtime routine needs to be satisfying. A child will resist being sent off to bed if she perceives that you are trying to be rid of her for the evening. She may resist a bedroom that is too remote, making her feel abandoned or scared, yet she needs to be far enough out of the mainstream of activity to drop off to sleep.

One way to determine a good bedtime is to see when your child naturally gets sleepy, yawns, becomes glassy-eyed or acts tired, as well as how she functions the next day with a given amount of sleep. You can then set bedtime so that she gets the optimum amount of sleep to function well. If you have one of those children who needs very little sleep, you can set up the expectation that she play with some toys in bed, look at books, or read (when she's older), so you can have sometime in the evenings without being "on duty." You can even explain to your child that you need this time.

Most children respond well to a routine for bedtime. It seems to condition them for sleep and helps to make them feel included in the family schedule. A bath, a certain number of stories, and a drink of warm milk might be satisfactory. When our son was about a year and a half old, a story, some warm milk, followed by three yawns— not one or two—was the signal that he was ready to go to bed.

Tucking in a doll or a teddy bear can distract a reluctant child from the act of actually going to bed herself. Sometimes putting on pajamas can involve a stall tactic by the child. A toy animal to "watch" her get ready for bed—or even to dress for bed first—can be helpful. Also, if getting dressed in the morning is a problem, having the child lay out clothes the night before can inspire cooperation. Some or all of the above. These little touches can be important, but it is also important, after all these things are considered, that you expect that the bedtime be honored. If the child keeps insisting on getting up or wanting another drink of water, it is time to problem-solve.

Questions you might ask are:

1. Has my child matured since we last set her bedtime?
2. Are we rushing through the bedtime routine so that she feels we are trying to get her out of sight?
3. Are the stories or routine scary or so stimulating that the child is fearful or wide awake?
4. Is her bedroom so remote that she feels frightened or abandoned?
5. Is her bedroom close to activity in the household and, perhaps a loud TV, so she cannot drop off to sleep?
6. Is her sleeping arrangement comfortable—not too hot or too cold, enough fresh air?
7. Is she physically tired, having enough activity and exercise during the day to make her feel sleepy?

This might sound like a lot of effort just to get a child to go to sleep, but it takes less time in the long run than a nightly battle. Perhaps more important, it turns what could be a stressful experience into a satisfying end to a busy day.

Since eating and sleeping are part of the everyday routine, it is worth every effort to try to work out any problems. Obviously, it eliminates a lot of unhappiness. Also, and perhaps even more important, any habits that children develop to manipulate their parents in these areas can carry over into other parent-child relationships. For many reasons it is an advantage to have both eating and sleeping activities go as smoothly and be as trouble-free as possible.

parents in these areas can carry over into other parent-child relationships. For many reasons it is an advantage to have both eating and sleeping activities go as smoothly and be as trouble-free as possible.

7

HANDLING ANGER: YOURS AND THEIRS

We all feel anger at times, adult and child alike. But, it is essential for us as parents to develop an understanding of anger and learn how to dissipate it, because anger left unresolved often overflows into our relationship with our children in a very unhealthy way. For example, we might overreact to something they do or lay blame and guilt, when perhaps the fault lies with us. It is imperative to get a handle on our own anger because to use preventive discipline successfully, a person has to be objective— very difficult or impossible when angry.

Understanding and Dealing With Anger

The important thing to recognize is that anger is a secondary reaction. The primary reaction comes from being frustrated or violated in some way—humiliated, insulted, ignored, or having our space invaded without permission. (For my ideas on the concept of "space," please see Chapter 2.) Think about the things which make you angry, and you will find that they most probably fall into one of these categories.

Usually anger is the result of some interaction with another person or persons, but sometimes it is caused by circumstances beyond anyone's control. In the latter case, you are not likely to feel as angry because you do not feel disrespected. I am thinking, for example, of a package that did not arrive on time because a storm slowed down the mail. However, if that same package was late because it was not sent on time, you feel let down, disrespected by the person responsible. In another scenario, a person may get angry with himself if he has not accomplished a certain task to his own satisfaction.

We can try to dissipate our own anger by deciphering the cause and dealing with it, either by talking to the offending person, accepting a situation that cannot be changed, or formulating a plan of action that might improve the circumstances. Often, just identifying the situation that is causing the anger makes it more manageable.

When a child misbehaves, parents often feel anger caused by one of the factors mentioned above: frustration or a violation of some kind. It seems as though the child has shown disrespect by not responding to our direction or disputing us. If we become angry, it is almost impossible to maintain enough objectivity to handle our own feelings and meet the challenge of getting at the cause of the child's misbehavior. As for the cause of the child's misbehavior, it is most likely the result of *his* anger at some situation over which he has no control. As parents, we can avoid the kinds of responses and situations that cause a child to get angry. Giving a positive direction rather than a demanding order can avoid one of the causes of child anger. In addition, a lot of frustration can be eliminated by a warning ahead of time for a change in activities, and despair can be avoided by helping with difficult tasks. When all else fails, empathy is very effective in soothing children when they are confronted with a situation beyond their control. Humiliation can be avoided by not scolding, especially in front of others, and by not down-grading a child's efforts.

After stopping the unwanted behavior in a positive way, correction in private in clear directions will help him know how to handle the situation next time. For example, when a child keeps interrupting your conversation with another adult, if you say, "What's the matter with you? How many times have I told you not to interrupt! That's very rude!" the child will feel inner anger at being put down and embarrassed. You will likely get an angry response or withdrawal. Instead you can say, "Please don't interrupt. We'll talk as soon as I'm through." Later in private you can say, "Next time I want you to wait until I'm through talking before you ask me something. Just come over and touch me on the arm, and I'll answer your question as soon as I can." Then, when you are in conversation the next time and the child touches you on the arm, answer the child as soon as possible. A child needs a prompt answer to an urgent question or problem, for children cannot be expected to wait long.

For the child, being ignored is one of the greatest frustrations of all, yet it is very common. Such treatment needs to be avoided at all costs with acknowledgment through listening and thoughtful responses. In some cases, just a nod of the head or a smile is all that is needed. If children are not noticed for positive things, they often misbehave so that they will not be ignored.

Ways To Avoid Temper Tantrums

Temper tantrums are dreaded events for parents of toddlers up to about three years of age. The kicking, screaming and uncontrolled crying are distressing and embarrassing, both to parent and child. Such tantrums are the acting out of extreme anger that children sometimes feel at situations beyond their control. I believe that these tantrums can be avoided, at least in part, by analyzing what causes them and doing something to counteract these causes.

A Dreaded Event

Some Causes of Temper Tantrums

- Leaving a pleasant situation
- Not getting or doing something wanted
- Not being able to work something
- Tiredness, hunger, or illness

Guidelines for avoiding trauma over leaving

One of the main causes of tantrums is having to leave a pleasant situation, often without warning. Grown-ups do not like that either, but we have developed more self control and have a sense of timing so that we know when something pleasant is coming to an end. Following are some guidelines to avoid a child's being upset when you and she have to leave:

Warn ahead of time. Let your child know a few minutes in advance that you'll have to leave, and why. Young children understand more words than they can express, and they often get the sense of the words by your inflection and body language. You can say, "We have to go soon because we need to pick up Mary at school. Let's help pick up the toys." Then after a few minutes, "We have to go now. Let's say good-bye."

Empathize. If the child cries or resists when it comes time to leave, even after all that preparation, try some empathy. You can say, "I know you want to stay, but we have to go now. We'll come back another day." (Add this last only if you know that it's a real possibility.)

Distract. You can say, "Here's a book for you to look at on the way to pick up Mary," or "Please carry this bag for Mommy until we get to the car." Young children have short attention spans, so they are easy to distract.

Ideas for avoiding problems when not getting or doing something wanted

Tantrums caused by a child's not getting a material item can be minimized by laying a solid groundwork beforehand by not getting him everything he asks for and by teaching respect for another's property. If a child picks up an item in the store and says, "Can I have this?" or, "I want this," there is already a crisis in the making since physical possession has taken place. Take time to establish that he can point, then ask, but that he is not to pick up anything that is someone else's property. This is a very valuable lesson to learn and can aid in avoiding many other problems. If a child asks properly for something that you do not think he should have, you can say, "No, I can't buy that for you," and give a reason. "You already have one," "It's too expensive," or "You need to be older," are all valid reasons, if true. Reasons need to make sense to both parent and child.

Tantrums brought on when a child cannot do something he wants to do can be lessened by using "No" sparingly. This does not mean letting the child do whatever he wants. It means saying "Yes" when possible, because usually what a child wants to do is all right. If most of our answers are yes, the occasional no is easier to accept. However, to be most effective our no needs a good reason, a consistent application and follow-through. When a child knows what to expect, frustration and, hence, fuel for tantrums are much less.

Ways to avoid frustration at not being able to work something

When possible, you can just put away the toy or activity he cannot work for a few weeks or months until the child has the coordination to handle it. In the case of something that must be used, such as a coat with a zipper, you can help as necessary before a feeling of defeat sets in. The way for a child to avoid frustration is to be able to succeed, and it is our job as parents to make each activity or task manageable.

Coping with tiredness, hunger or illness

If the child is unable to remedy the situation of being tired, hungry or ill, a tantrum may follow, since the situation is beyond his control. The way to avoid such tantrums is obvious but not always easy, especially when there are other schedules to consider. Respecting a child's need for rest is sometimes hard to accomplish. For toddlers, a stroller that allows a tired child to rest or even sleep is an important help. When our son was about a year and a half old, he had an old-fashioned metal stroller that could not be adjusted for sleeping. However, there was a basket in back in which I kept a small pillow. When he got tired he whisked the pillow from the basket to the tray in front of the seat, put his head down and went to sleep. Staving off hunger pangs is not such a problem; a box of crackers and some juice can do wonders in such emergencies. Sickness may be minor and treatable at home, or it may require a doctor.

The bottom line is that we, as parents, can help avoid the frustrations and resulting anger that causes most tantrums. They can become rare occurrences, or not happen at all. If, in spite of all our efforts, tantrums happen often and are extreme, it might be a sign of a serious problem that needs professional help.

In conclusion, anger in both adults and children can be distressing and debilitating. It is eminently worthwhile to put a great deal of thought and effort into learning to handle anger in a positive way. It makes for more fulfilled adults and adds to satisfying interrelationships between parents and children.

PART THREE

SHORT CUTS TO GOOD BEHAVIOR

8

FOCUS ON TODDLERS AND PRESCHOOLERS

"Aren't they cute?"you hear people say about toddlers and preschoolers. But there is the very real problem of caring for young children to keep them healthy, happy and safe, and letting you have some peace of mind, too. We have to keep them under control and supervised while they are too young to have developed adequate inner controls. We need to teach them discipline while giving them some control over their lives.

Some ideas follow for meeting special circumstances that come up with the young child. These approaches are compatible with the principles of attention, respect and empathy, the basic elements of preventive discipline. While many of these ideas concerning young children apply to older children as well, following these guidelines when your children are at a young age will allow the best chance for good results, both now and later.

Safety Rules

As parents we are responsible for the physical safety of our children when they are too young to take care of themselves. It is a matter of respect, as well as common sense, to do for them what they are not mature enough to do for themselves. Safety rules are an essential part of preventive discipline, in that the child gradually learns what actions are safe and acceptable without constantly being told what to do and not to do. It is related to setting limits before the event to help the child know what is expected and adds greatly to acceptable behavior.

I found it useful to make a set of rules which helped keep a safe environment without constantly thinking through each situation. I'd like to share with you the safety rules that helped me:

In General

• Supervise toddlers at all times. Know what they are doing and where they are every minute. Do not leave a baby or toddler alone in the house or car.

• Be very careful who supervises the children when they are at especially vulnerable stages, as they are from when they begin walking until about the age of three. The care giver might not be alert to the constant vigil necessary. When my son was a toddler, I asked a friend to watch him for a few minutes while I went into an apartment to see a piece of furniture for sale. When I came back, my son was nowhere to be seen. With my heart in my throat, I went behind the apartment building and there he was, toddling toward the street! I never again asked a friend to watch my children while they were at a vulnerable age.

In the Car and Walking

- Do not let children under about ten years of age out of a car on the opposite side of the street from their destination; conversely, do not pick them up on the opposite side of the street. We have all heard of a child's being struck by an oncoming car as he crossed the   street to go to or from school.

- Have the children get in and out of the car on the sidewalk side, never on the street side.

- Insist that children not be noisy, yell, or otherwise distract the driver.

- Have children walk with you across streets and through parking lots. Never let them run.

I had the following additional rules for myself in the days before mandatory car restraint seats for children. I include them here because they still have relevance. Also, it shows some additional advantages of having car seats besides the safety factor in an accident.

- Check that all doors are closed solidly when children get in and out of any car. This avoids the chance of their falling out of the car door. (I saw a child fall out of a car once; it is an indelible memory.)

- Do not allow children to lean out car windows or lean on doors.

- Do not let young children close car doors when other young children are getting in or out of the car. It is too hard to watch for everyone's fingers.

In the Home

- Put all poisonous and other dangerous things up high, out of reach, and preferably locked up.

- Encourage relatives whom your children visit to also put all poisonous and dangerous things out of reach.

- Regularly turn all handles of pots and pans on the stove in, so that no handle sticks out over the edge of the stove.

- Keep cords of electric coffee pots and other electric appliances out of reach, so they will not accidentally be pulled over.

- Keep anything hazardous back from the edge of counters.

- Store all sharp knives in a safe place and keep them out of reach when in use, such as when carving a roast.

- Put a folding gate at the top *and* bottom of all long flights of stairs and keep gates secured when children are around. I remember my distress at hearing one of our twins bump her head three times as she fell down a wooden flight of stairs. We were all downstairs when she decided to go up by herself. (And after that, we installed gates at the bottom of stairs, too.)

- Have a soft rug at the bottom of the stairs to the basement, which usually has a cement floor—in case the gate is not secured and the child falls. In fact, it is wise to have a soft surface at the bottom of all flights of stairs.

- Do not allow children to climb on tables or counters or bounce on beds or sofas. I learned the hard way. My son at age four was bouncing on the couch with a friend at her house. He catapulted into the air backwards, breaking the glass top of a coffee table. Result: a cut on the back of his head, lots of blood, and a big scare.

- Remove any furniture with sharp points or glass tops that could break if fallen on.

- Put any broken glass into a cardboard box or other container and into the trash immediately. I learned the hard way on this one, too. One of the twins at about seven was roller skating in the garage when she knocked over a jar, breaking it. I swept it into an open box on one side of the garage. On the next round she skated right into the box, hands first. Lots of blood again, and a scar that she carries to this day as a result of that preventable accident.

- Attach high bookcases or shelves to the wall to avoid their falling over should a child climb up on them, or if there is an earthquake.

- Do not leave any toys or other items so small they might be swallowed within reach of small children.

- Be sure bath water is not so hot that it scalds small children and that they cannot turn on water that might be too hot. Baths for this age group need good supervision.

Most of these rules are self evident and widely publicized, but some are ones that I have put into practice as a result of being involved in, witnessing, or hearing about particular accidents. These rules are not only useful in providing for the physical safety of young children; they carry over into self discipline and good safety habits for the children as they get older.

Suitcase With a Surprise

Invaluable ideas can be learned from friends. I learned one such idea from a friend who always gave her children a "suitcase with a surprise" when her children's bedtime rolled around and she was entertaining an adult gathering. The children would say goodnight to us guests, and we heard nothing more from them. The guests were impressed with how "well-behaved" the children were. This provides an excellent example of how preventive discipline can work through setting up a situation ahead of time that is satisfying to all.

A Suitcase With A Surprise

The idea of having a "suitcase with a surprise" worked for us, too. I bought little suitcases for each child, and whenever we had company for the evening I would prepare the suitcases ahead of time. In each one I put a couple of toys and books that had not been looked at for a while and some treats, like a couple of cookies, some nuts, and a box of raisins. (While sweets and fruit are not good after tooth brushing as a rule, I do not think a special treat is harmful if allowed now and then.) When it came time to go to bed, the children came down in their pajamas to say goodnight to the company, a necessary part of the routine. Then they trotted off to bed, each with suitcase in hand.

The agreement with the children was that they could open the suitcases only when they were in their beds, play as long as they wanted, then go to sleep without calling us. Our company was always impressed, and we did not have to worry about difficulties getting the children to settle down. This worked for our children when they were toddlers, preschoolers, and even primary schoolers. One spin-off that we did not expect: the children loved for us to have company so they could have their "suitcase with a surprise!"

Travel Tips

Generally, a trip is something to which everyone looks forward with pleasure. It is a chance for us to see something new, visit family or friends, or just have a change in routine. Traveling with children adds an extra dimension. It can make the trip a memorable family adventure, a barely tolerable experience, or a nightmare.

To guarantee that the extra dimension is a delightful one, we have to provide for the children's needs, both physical and psychological, just as though we were at home, but under more difficult circumstances. It is harder to anticipate and meet these needs when we are out of our routine and the means for satisfying them are not easily at hand. It almost goes without saying that the younger the children, the harder it is for them to put off having their needs satisfied. Even though the suggestions in this section apply to all ages, their application starts with young children.

That is why I have included it here. To have a good trip, we need to think of the principles of preventive discipline: attention, respect and empathy. We can give attention by having conversation, playing games and providing toys. Respect, especially, can be shown by meeting both the physical and psychological needs of the children. Empathy can be shown when they tire of traveling and begin asking, "Are we there yet?" You can say, "I bet you wish we were there now. It will be a little while yet. How about reading this story?"

The better you anticipate and provide for the inevitable needs, the smoother the trip—and the better the memories. Following are some considerations you might find helpful.

- Have snacks and drinks handy.
- Stop for meals before children are desperately hungry. If you wait until hunger sets in, it is too late to avoid fussy, unhappy children. (I remember well!)
- Provide an opportunity for enough rest while traveling or by stopping overnight.
- Stop at intervals for exercise. Lunch at a park gives a chance to let off steam. A mid-afternoon stop at a playground can be good for everyone.
- To fight boredom, have games and toys. For a trip of several days, a new little trinket or toy each day is helpful. In fact, children will look forward to it.
- Give special attention to the children by playing games appropriate to their ages or by singing songs. (See Appendix for suggestions.)
- Some children are sensitive to motion, which can lead to a fussy or sick child. Slowing down a bit on curves and rough roads can do wonders to soothe a queasy stomach for children—and for adults, too, incidentally.
- In general, plan the itinerary so that it is suitable to the children's ages, in regard to both needs and interests.

Some people's solution to travel is to leave the children home in someone else's care. This is probably best if the trip is unsuitable for children, such as an all-adult or business trip. However, if a trip can be adapted to the ages and needs of the children, both the parents and children are enriched and can enjoy sharing their experiences.

9

THE ELEMENTARY AND MIDDLE SCHOOL YEARS

This is the period in which children are usually the most responsive to guidance and influence over their behavior. They have a sense of fairness and reason, have learned to put off gratification—at least a little—and are, in general, industrious and receptive to trying and learning new things. The following situations are by no means all that occur, but they point out some ideas and philosophies that have worked for me. They may help make these years smoother for you, too. These elementary and middle school situations are by no means exclusive to the particular ages covered, but they do begin here. Good habits formed at this time can promote self discipline and carry over into the teen years.

Tea Time

A treasured custom that I learned from an English acquaintance was the value of a "tea time." She told me she always had tea with her children when they came home from school. Not being English, I modified the idea into an American snack time. I would drop everything when my children arrived home from school and we would have milk and cookies, or some such.

Our tea time had several benefits that I did not expect. The children always came right home after school, bursting through the door with papers to show, tales to tell, or a problem to share. We had a chance right then to deal with any traumas or share in the delight of a success. Two instances come to mind during the high school years when I needed to commiserate with one daughter and congratulate the other. I was really glad we had the time built into our routine, for each instance was very important. Since the girls were twins, the problems were magnified because I could not say that one was older so had maturity on her side. However, even when ages are different, there are still hurt feelings to deal with.

In the first instance, our daughter who played French horn came excitedly through the door to announce that she had won a place in the California State Honor Band. Our other daughter, a trombonist, reported tearfully that she did not make it. I was put in the difficult situation of congratulating one daughter and consoling the other! Somehow we got through it. I am sure it was best to deal with the situation right away.

Another day the twins came home with one again wearing a long face and the other an ecstatic one. (Fortunately, the disappointed one was the elated one in the other example.) The disappointed daughter launched into an explanation. She had physical education first period at which time she broke the school record for the 100-yard dash. Her twin had physical education sixth period, at which time she broke her sister's record! One had been a record holder for just part of a day, but at least we got the whole story out right away and reconciled the hurt feelings with some well-placed empathy.

An additional benefit of tea time that I did not realize until much later was that we were establishing excellent lines of communication, a necessity for good behavior. The good communication skills paved the way for talking at any time (and I emphasize at any time) about problems or disagreements.

Of course, circumstances have changed since I was raising my children. Many mothers now work and are not home to greet their children when school is over. However, I believe that the same benefits can be derived from tea time by setting aside the first five or ten minutes that the working mother and her children arrive home from day care or the mother gets home and relieves the in-home sitter. Putting away groceries and starting dinner will not suffer measurably by waiting a few minutes, and the lift from having a snack plus undivided time with the children provides a real boost for all.

I have often thought of that Englishwoman, whom I knew only briefly when my first child was just a baby, and have been grateful for her passing comment. It led to one of our most valued family customs.

Taming The TV

Many a battle is fought over TV—what to watch, how much, and when. Problems can be minimized if we get our roles straight. We as parents have the responsibility to decide what we think is all right to watch, the maximum time to spend in front of the TV, and how late a child can stay up to watch. I believe that the best results occur when the child has a choice of programs within those limits. Making these decisions about TV watching fits in with the principles of preventive discipline, with limits being set ahead of time. Moreover, attention, respect and empathy are part of the process.

Our first responsibility is to be aware of the contents of the programs our children see, not allowing them to watch those we think might be harmful to the values we are trying to teach. This is easier said than done, but it goes more smoothly if we start evaluating what our children watch right from the beginning. We need to state good reasons for our decisions, or we will get lots of resistance. (We will get some, no matter how good our reasons.) Parents have to decide what criteria to follow and then be consistent. My husband and I felt that programs with a lot of realistic violence were harmful, including cartoons. (The effect of cartoons is controversial, incidentally. Some believe that children are not influenced by them.) Our evaluation of what was undesirable covered the majority of modern detective series but not most Westerns, which seemed to us more make-believe. There were always plenty of programs to watch that were entertaining, yet not harmful. In addition there were, and still are, fascinating educational programs, such as *Sesame Street*, *Reading Rainbow*, and the *National Geographic* programs, each appealing to a different age.

The conditions for monitoring TV have changed a lot in recent years. It was much easier with only one TV in the home. However, even though most families now have two or more TVs, it is very important to know what the children are watching, joining them for at least a program or two of any series to be sure we approve. The cable channels now available help ensure choices that are suitable. For example, I have heard parents singing the praises of the Disney channel and Nickelodeon for reliable programming. The new voluntary rating system is helpful, too, in deciding whether something is suitable for the children to watch. However, I think it is still best if parents watch the programs to see for themselves.

The placement of the TV is important, too. To help children form good habits, I suggest keeping sets out of bedrooms, where they might interfere with homework, and out of the dining room, where it could be a temptation to watch during meals.

Another thing that we need to help our children limit is the number of hours watched. Too much time in front of TV keeps children too inactive and more inclined to merely absorb impressions rather than respond to other people, and stimuli. One way to limit the time is to figure out a reasonable number of hours per day—perhaps allowing more on Saturday and Sunday—then let the children choose which programs they most want to watch from those of which you approve and which do not run too late. Our children liked the Saturday morning programs which went from 8 to 12. We thought that two hours was plenty of TV, so we gave them a choice of two hours of programming from those we approved and they liked most. They seemed happy with that arrangement.

In the case of older children, it is important for them to plan their watching to fit in with their responsibilities, such as homework or chores. Telling children they cannot watch until their work is done can produce a lot of resistance, and they miss the chance to learn how to plan their time. If they can't make a plan and stick to it, however, we may have to help them. We could say, "You said you planned to start your homework after this program." An observation such as this usually gets little resistance; it acts as a reminder of an agreement the child made. A statement like, "Start your homework now that the program is over" would likely he interpreted as nagging, which more children do resist.

Something that helps children limit their TV watching is to suggest, and have available, a lot of other things to do—books to read, games to play, sports equipment to use, and group activities to participate in. Examples are recreation programs for preschoolers and team sports for older children. Not only is it wise to have alternatives to TV available, it helps if parents actively join the children when appropriate, such as in Scouting.

A third responsibility we have in connection with TV is to determine how late children can stay up to watch. This depends on how much sleep each child needs to function well, whether it's a school night in the case of older children, and whether there's a special occasion or program involved. It's a limit that needs constant reevaluation since the needs for sleep change as a child matures.

A further dimension is added today by video tapes and video games played on the computer. However, the same criteria apply in limiting their use as in watching TV: suitable subjects, a limited time spent in front of the screen, and an optimum bedtime. Used ideally, video tapes and games can enhance the life of a child. Children are quite accepting of the TV limits we set if we have understandable reasons. They will still press to see a certain series or program because "everyone watches it," but if we have a reasonable approach they will accept the limits. You can say, "I know other families watch that, but in our family we don't because. . ." and explain your reasons. They get the message that we are concerned for their welfare which gives them a certain security, at the same time building family identity. Children will even brag to others that their parents won't let them watch certain programs. One popular program that we refused to let the children watch was "The Three Stooges." We explained that the humor was centered around actions we did not think were funny, like hitting someone over the head, giving the hot foot with a match, or laughing when characters fell. Right or wrong, we felt it was not in our family values to laugh at someone else's misfortune, even though many considered the antics humorous. I am sure our children saw the program when they visited friends, but they knew where we stood as a family.

I found that limiting TV had an unexpected result. It helped the children be more selective in other things and not feel they always had to go along with their peers. That is a powerful asset in growing up in this ever more complex society.

Making Homework Happen

I have friends who say, "I can't come tonight because I have to sit with my children while they do their homework." If that is a routine occurrence, I believe that both parents and children are shortchanging themselves. Homework should be at a level that the average child can handle. Ideally we then guide the child toward the self discipline to get it done on time. The child can feel successful, and parents can live their own lives. If the work is too difficult for the child, a conference with the teacher is called for. Perhaps the teacher is going too fast for the class or your child needs some special tutoring.

We parents do have responsibility for setting up conditions for successful management of homework. It is an example of the positive approach in preventive discipline. We need to provide a quiet place for each child to call his own that is suitable for homework—a desk or table, good light, a comfortable chair, and space for books and paper. Some children prefer to do their homework on the kitchen table amidst the household noise, as my daughters did, but they still need a spot to keep their things, a place to which they can retreat if necessary. We also need to work out a mutually agreed upon schedule that allows enough time for homework and enough sleep to function well the following day. This involves limiting TV, sports and other play. It is not necessary to say, "You can't watch TV (or play ball) until all your homework is done." Rather, we can ask, "When are you planning to do your homework?" When a youngster establishes a plan, get him to stick to it with reminders. Also, help him think about starting big projects, like reports, ahead of time so he is not faced with an impossible last-minute task.

Making Homework Happen

I do not mean that we should never help children with homework. Sometimes there is a problem that cannot be worked out, they need help planning a project or gathering resources, or they want advice on a paper.

One project I helped with quite a lot was a science project in which one of our daughters decided to hatch some duck eggs. The first challenge was to find a source of fertilized duck eggs. After getting the eggs, we made an incubator from a cardboard box, a light bulb on a cord, and a thermometer. Hatching ducks is quite exacting, and the whole process takes 30 days instead of the 21 days for chicks. The night before the eggs were to hatch, there was a storm that knocked out the electricity! We kept the incubator as warm as possible with blankets, but after that only one egg bobbed in water, a sign that a live duck was inside. Finally after several hours, the duckling burst the shell open and hatched. (How that big duckling ever fit in that little egg amazed us.) Appropriately our daughter named it "Super Duck."

On other occasions, too, we helped the children gather the necessary resources for reports or projects. This sometimes necessitated trips to the library, store or craft shop. In each case, we expected them to do the work. Our part was to give support and to help them gather the needed tools.

While I believe it is good to help with homework or projects where help is needed, what I do not think is wise is to routinely sit with children while they do their homework, organize it for them, and then go over all their work. They not only fail to learn self discipline and ways to manage their time, but they also get a feeling of inadequacy. Ideally, our goal as parents is to help our children be self directed and self sufficient, giving them help and support as needed to attain this goal.

Kids' Chores A Chore?

"It's harder to get the kids to do their chores than to do them myself," is an oft-heard complaint. Yet, is if fair for the parents to do all of the work, and is it fair for the children not to learn some responsibility for the family chores? On both counts, I believe the answer is a resounding no. It is an essential part of preventive discipline to teach responsibility, so that children learn to carry their weight and thereby avoid the war of words over the sharing of work. The question is, how do you get children to cooperate?

It is ideal, of course, to start early with children and expect them to take on some responsibilities, like picking up their toys and hanging up their coats. As they get older, they can be expected to do more extensive chores. The greatest difficulty comes when the chore is not just picking up after themselves, but is a family need.

The first step for us as parents is to establish the fact that family chores are a family responsibility; next we need to get some input from the children about which chores they will take on and, more important, when they will be done. If they have some say in the planning, they will be much more willing to cooperate. In the final analysis, of course, we are the judges as to what is an appropriate work list and schedule.

Some appropriate chores as children reach school age are setting the table, cleaning up the dishes, making their own beds, cleaning their rooms, taking out the trash, and mowing the lawn. In some families, children have the same chores all the time, and in others, they trade around. It does not matter, as long as it is agreed upon. In our family, division of labor was pretty traditional—our son mowed the lawn and did the outside things, besides making his bed, and our daughters took care of the indoor jobs. That is the way they wanted to divide up the chores. Contrary to popular belief, their choice of chores did not have a carry-over into adult life. They all do the full range of family chores, both inside and out.

If someone falls behind in his responsibilities, reminders in the form of questions are useful. You can ask, "When do you plan to mow the lawn?" which is what I would say to my son. He would answer something like, "This afternoon," and it would happen. This approach allows the child to save face and do the job without feeling scolded. If you need it done sooner than the child plans, you can give an "I" message by saying, "I'd really like the yard looking nice by this afternoon." Another type of reminder that does not get resistance is, "Time to do the dishes," instead of, "Do those dishes, right now."

Flexibility on everyone's part is essential in order to fit in special needs. If a child has a particular event coming up that interferes with a chore, we can ask him when he plans to work it in. This assumes that we expect him to carry out his responsibilities and that we also expect him to plan how to do it. Both show respect for the person and should get a positive response.

Sharing family chores is really another way of showing mutual respect. This is an essential element for a family's getting along happily as a unit, and it is another invaluable quality to carry over into adult life.

Making A Monetary Allowance Pay

"Learn by doing," is a well-known phrase coined by the educator John Dewey. Children can learn a great deal about the value of money by having a regular allowance and handling the money entirely by themselves. It does not need to be a big allowance, but it needs to be regular and suitable for the child's age.

School age is a good time to start an allowance. I believe that to be most beneficial, there should be "no strings attached." The child will learn the most by being able to do whatever he wants with it. I do not think it is helpful to insist that a certain portion be saved. He will soon learn on his own that to get something big, he has to put off gratification and save his money. As far as saving for a college education, a preoccupation of many parents, this can better come much later when a child is old enough to work outside the home.

The young child with his first allowance may spend all of it the first day on a toy or candy, but he will soon learn that he does not have enough left to buy some other prized object. The realization on his part that he has to save for a bigger treasure is one of the most valuable things he can learn. The child not only learns to put off gratification, but he also develops an idea of the value of money. It is a wonderful foundation for living within a budget later.

In establishing an allowance, we need to be clear on just what we expect the child to pay for. In the case of a very young child, it is best to have him responsible for every few things, for example, toys and treats, so he can handle the choices and the planning. A school-age child can be responsible for more, such as pencils for school, entertainment and presents.

The amount of the allowance is always a difficult decision. The going rate for peers can be some guide, but a more important consideration is how it fits in with the family budget and what the parents think is appropriate for the age of the child. I believe it is good to keep the amount on the low side to inspire careful planning, appreciation of the value of money, and encouragement for older children to earn extra money by doing odd jobs, such as baby-sitting and mowing lawns.

There is sometimes a temptation to give a child extra money if he runs out. However, we defeat the purpose of his learning to plan if this is done. We might make a loan to help a child over a rough spot, but if we do, it is best to record the amount and insist that at least some be paid back out of the next allowance, recording this, too. Then, no more loans until the balance is paid off. One of the best lessons that can be learned in connection with handling money is to pay back loans promptly and in full. If the child runs out of money often, it may be that the allowance is too low or we are asking him to cover too much of his expenses. The amount of the allowance needs to be constantly reevaluated. Every family has to decide its own philosophy on the subject of paying children for chores. We decided not to pay for chores because we felt that they were a shared family responsibility. When our son baby-sat his younger sisters, we left a special treat, like a pie or some ice cream, to reward all of them for co-operating with each other. Their weekly allowance went up as they assumed more advanced responsibilities, such as staying home without an outside sitter.

Giving the children a regular allowance had several valuable benefits. There was an understanding about money that eliminated constant requests. Also, they had control over their own resources, which eliminated a lot of the common causes of friction between children and parents. Finally, the children learned to plan their spending and live within a budget. This really helped them be financially independent later on, a goal of all parents for their children.

The Clothing Allowance

As children get older and have definite ideas about what they want to wear, buying clothes can be a bottom-less pit, both in trips to the store and to the bank. It can also be the cause of many disagreements and arguments. One reason is that there is often a wide gap between needs and wants. Children need clothes to keep warm and to be reasonably in style, but some want to be fashion plates.

One way we limited the confrontations over clothes was to have a clothing allowance. I got this idea when our twin daughters started middle school and showed the unmistakable signs of approaching their teen years. They had gotten so they would not wear any clothes I picked out for them. Even if the choice was theirs, they would often change their minds about what clothes they would wear and start badgering me for new ones. Something had to done!

The clothing allowance proved to solve most of the problems. The way we handled it was really a matter of bookkeeping. Their father and I, with the children's input, decided upon the amount of the allowance. We gave them cash when they made their purchases, and I kept the books so we would all know the expenditures and the balance.

Deciding on the dollar amount to set for the clothing allowance depended on what clothes were included, what the cost of acceptable clothing was, and the level of the family income at the time. It was also influenced by the ages of the children, since the need for a variety of clothes went up with age. Together with the children we figured out an allowance for needs and let them know that anything above that was their financial responsibility. They could use gift money, their allowances, or do odd jobs to earn some extra funds. Fortunately, the children were old enough to take on little jobs outside the home when they began to want certain extra clothes.

With the clothing allowance, the children chose their clothes more carefully, took better care of them, and valued more highly any additional clothes they bought with their own money. They even learned to use good thrift shops to advantage.

One of the decisions we had to make was what to include in the clothing allowance. We decided to include everything but coats and shoes, the former because they were such a major purchase, and the latter because we did not want the children to skimp on the quality of shoes. We also bought special garments such as graduation clothes, since they were variable and hard to include in an overall plan. When the children got things like pajamas and socks given to them as presents for birthdays and Christmas, they really appreciated them as gifts since those items did not, then, have to come out of their clothing allowance. Incidentally, when our son, now grown, was reading over my manuscript, his strong reaction was, "I don't remember *liking* clothes as gifts!"

I thought back and realized that we did not start the clothing allowance until he was in high school, so he did not grow up with the tradition. He was polite, however, and never complained about such gifts.

Another thing the children learned through the clothing allowance was to plan very carefully so that outfits were coordinated, served several purposes, and were lasting. I was always available for advice, but the choice was theirs. Another good way we helped the children stretch their clothing allowance was to encourage them to make some of their own clothes. Our daughters went this route. Although girls are more prone to do their own sewing, there is no reason why boys could not be encouraged to tailor and sew as well.

We had a special problem with our twin daughters that could also be a problem for siblings close in age or size. They often wanted the same thing, so I made it a rule to always shop with them separately, so they could pick out something different. However, much later when they were older and home from college, I took them shopping together to buy dresses for their birthday. I thought that after years of dressing differently, I did not need to worry about shopping separately. They carefully looked through the possibilities on their own, tried them on, and made their choices. Imagine our surprise to find they had picked exactly the same dresses!

We started the clothing allowance in the middle school years, at least for the girls, and continued right through college. It had many advantages for us. Besides having an understood limit to clothes for which we would pay, the allowance provided a valuable learning experience for the children and gave us another chance to interact in a positive way.

10

LIVING WITH TEENAGERS

This is the stage many parents dread most. Groundwork laid when children are younger, from toddlers on, can help create a smoother road for relations between teenagers and parents. What teenagers want most is autonomy in which they can make some of their own decisions, but with the security of parental guidance. The basic elements of attention, respect and empathy which we have talked about in preventive discipline, plus the experience of making decisions appropriate to their age through the years, help both teenager and parent ease into this difficult period.

"But my child is already a teenager, so it's too late to start something new," someone might say. It is not too late to start, but it is harder because the groundwork has not been laid and the approach is new to both teen and parent. However, preventive discipline can still be most helpful in developing a good relationship in which teenagers have the autonomy to make more of their own decisions, but have the guidance and limits of thoughtful, caring parents.

The Generation Gap

The teenage years, when children begin to strongly assert themselves, can be a time of tension for both teenagers and parents. However, tensions can be lessened if we think about the causes of this generation gap and try to remedy them. I think the main causes are:

1. older children want to be treated more like adults;
2. some social values change as times change; and
3. teenagers want to push the limits, developing their own values or adopting new ones, not always in sync with the family values they have known.

Children like to have some control over their lives, and when they reach the preteen and teenage years they insist on it, even to the point of being rebellious. They are becoming adults, though hesitantly at first. They have to break away from their parents and become individuals in control of their own lives in order to do so.

The necessary breaking away from parental control can be accomplished more smoothly by giving a child gradual control over appropriate parts of his life as he grows, from a toddler on. At first the limits are very constricted. There are only a few things a toddler can decide; sharing his own toys is one example. As children grow older, their limits broaden and might include such things as choosing which clothes to wear from several suitable outfits. Later they can choose which clothes to buy, plan their homework time, and decide how to spend their own money. If the limits are gradually expanded and children's decision-making and responsibility for their decisions are expanded accordingly, there is not much to rebel against, at least as far as parents are concerned.

Some parents interpret this expansion of children's control over their own lives as letting them do as they please. This does not have to be the case at all. Parents still can be in charge as long as a child lives at home and is dependent financially. Parents can still set the values and the general household rules.

Now comes the question of a difference in values between parents and teenagers. Parents often believe that what was appropriate for them when they were growing up is appropriate now, for their own children. It may not be. Perhaps it was not the best even then, and it certainly bears thinking through a generation later. It is important, however difficult, to be truly open-minded. Perhaps you will decide the value with which you grew up is still the best one. Whatever the conclusion, you can insist on it in all good conscience if you have thought it through. Children may complain if your decision does not agree with what they want to do. However, in my experience, they will accept it if they know you have thought about the situation and have their welfare in mind. This is the case, even if their peers are allowed the privilege in question.

I remember one incident that involved an urgent request. Our son as an early teenager wanted to go to the local movie house with his friends on a Friday night. This particular theater was known for the bedlam that took place on that night each week—noise, jumping over the seats, lighting matches. We said, "No," because, as we told him, a person could not really see the movie in such chaos, and besides, it was dangerous. We offered to take him and his friends to some other theater whenever he wanted. He complained some, but later we overheard him bragging to some of his friends, "My parents won't *let* me go to that theater on Friday nights!"

In general, attitudes may differ between teenager and their parents in many areas. A few examples are what clothes are appropriate, how late to stay out, what parties or get-togethers are approved of, and choice of friends. It is important to have in mind a philosophy to guide you in decision-making about what you approve. The philosophy mentioned earlier can still apply; it is all right if it is safe, not harmful to health, and generally felt to be socially acceptable.

If denial of an activity or privilege does not fit into one of the above categories, the reason for denial is hard to justify and equally hard for teenagers to accept. For example, if your child wants to wear a casual outfit to an event like a reception that you think calls for more formal clothes, you might reconsider if your child points out that casual clothes are in keeping with the way her age group dresses for such occasions. Applying the test mentioned above, the more informal dress would be safe, not harmful to health, and is now socially acceptable, even if it was not when you were that age. I can remember once insisting that my daughters dress up for a classical concert and their dates arriving dressed very casually. I wished I had been more responsive to the girls' insistence that informal dress was acceptable. I would have been able to give my approval knowing that I had not given up my values of dressing appropriately, just modified them reasonably to suit the new era.

The time to be home at night is another example of a limit parents put on teenage children. Useful guidelines are to set the hour according to the child's age and the generally accepted limits for his peers. Each event also needs to be considered, so that the child has enough time to get home safely. If he complains about the set hour, it can be time for the parent to ask, "Why?" You might say, "Why does that time seem too early?" It may be that his peers stay out a little later, that he has to break up the gathering if he leaves earlier, or that he feels his privileges are not commensurate with his age. Perhaps it is time to reevaluate. Is it bad for his health or morals to stay out a little later? Has he matured since you last set the time? Perhaps you can readjust your expectations without compromising your values.

The value of asking why if there is a disagreement is that it gives you room to negotiate. Neither you nor your child has to give in or lose face. It avoids a lot of resistance and rebellion because we are showing understanding and respect. Living with children, especially teenagers, demands that we constantly reevaluate whether our expectations are realistic and valid for the child's age and for the times.

Teenagers typically want to test the limits; they also begin forming some of their own values. We have the most success if we show respect for teenagers' ideas by being open-minded and non-judgmental. To be accepted, what we say in our response needs to be straightforward and make good sense.

Dealing in ideas with teenagers is a lot more difficult than with younger children. We want our teens to start thinking for themselves, yet incorporate the values we think are most important. Many subjects come up with teenagers, though it is not always possible to develop a constructive dialogue, especially if we have not begun to have such dialogues early. There is a potential difference of values concerning smoking, drinking, drugs, money and sex, to name a few. We have a much better chance of talking together about these topics if we have developed a habit of having discussions in which the participants truly listen to each other without a preconceived idea of the outcome.

Perhaps the hardest subject to talk about with teenagers is sex. In some families it is never or rarely mentioned, though it should be. Values concerning sex could be brought up while discussing such issues as drinking at parties or staying out too late at night. There is the danger of getting more sexually involved than planned in either of these circumstances.

Perhaps the teenager will say it is part of the mores among his age group now to have sex, and that he does not see what is objectionable; it is natural, pleasurable, and accepted. You might say, "I agree that times have changed and that it's more accepted, but I have a major concern. A person needs to be extremely responsible to protect against AIDS and pregnancy." Then you might go into a discussion of adequate protection, even offering some of the excellent pamphlets and other material available. Or, you may feel that sex for teenagers, especially of high school age, is unacceptable.

You could make the above point and then go on to say, "You have some very valid ideas, but there are some things that really worry me. Protection against pregnancy and AIDS is available but not completely reliable. The price of an unwanted pregnancy is to short-circuit your goals, and in the case of AIDS, to short-circuit your life. There is also a strong emotional side to sex. It is hard for a young person to adjust to the ups and downs of a serious relationship. Young people are wise to let themselves have some time to mature before getting deeply involved."

Another value strongly felt is that sex should be put off until marriage. You might say, "Even though sexual mores are different now than a few years ago, it is an expression of love that I believe is best saved for marriage. Sex is a special relationship to cherish with only the person you marry. Another very real reason for abstinence is that there is no worry about pregnancy before marriage, and in this day and age, AIDS."

After you have discussed the reasons for your beliefs, whatever they may be, just let the matter drop! Teenagers will mull over your values and what you have said and will incorporate them with the ones they are forming, if they are not preached at and badgered.

The teenage years of our children can provide exciting and dramatic challenges. We are watching them and, we hope, helping them grow into adulthood. There are always problems, but it is the way they are solved that is important. The ideal is to meet each problem so that it is a learning, but not a damaging, experience.

If we are diligent in giving teenagers some control over their own lives, yet guide them through difficult decisions, we can enjoy the growing up years. It is the culmination of raising our children from infancy to adulthood.

Keys To The Car: Rite Of Passage

There comes a time in a teenager's life when the dream is to have the keys to the car. Being able to drive is a symbol of freedom and of growing up—a kind of modern rite of passage. This strikes fear in the hearts of many parents. It represents a tangible breaking away from parental control and can also be a real danger to the teenager.

Driving is a heavy responsibility. Every step possible needs to be taken to assure that it can be handled well. Here are some ideas to help make this momentous event a positive experience instead of a negative one for both parent and teenager. Working with a teenager learning to drive takes as much skill in preventive discipline as a parent can muster, since it needs lots of positive attention, respect in a difficult situation, and empathy for the learner.

First, take advantage of every aid for learning to drive. Most high schools have courses in safety education, which in some cases include behind-the-wheel experience. (The latter had to be eliminated in many schools because of budget constraints. In the absence of such programs, commercial driving schools can be used.) In some states, a good grade point average in all subjects translates into a lower auto insurance rate, providing a good incentive for doing well in school.

Keys to the Car

Second, it helps tremendously in developing good drivers to insist that the teenager have plenty of practice behind the wheel before getting a license—more than they can get during driver education and while the minimum permit period is in effect. Usually, as soon as students finish the driver education course and they are of age, they want their licenses. If they pass both the written and driving tests, they can legally get one. However, I think it is a serious mistake for most teenagers to get their licenses that soon. Driving is a skill that takes experience and practice, and nothing can take the place of time behind the wheel in all kinds of circumstances. It is important for new drivers to have enough driving experience so that the mechanical aspects of driving and the judgment of distance become automatic. It frees the driver to be alert to traffic, react well in an emergency, and be generally aware of all that is involved in driving a car.

In the case of our three children we believed that, in addition to the above, they should learn to drive both of our cars, automatic and stick shift, and that they should have experience driving at night and on freeways. This enabled them to drive any car, anytime, anywhere—and assured more time behind the wheel. In regard to the exact timing for applying for the driver's license, their father said, "You can get your license when I feel comfortable," referring primarily to safety. They would periodically ask, "How long before I can get my license?" Their father would repeat, "When I feel comfortable." That was the best decision we made. It not only gave the children plenty of supervised practice, but it gave us a chance to talk about the responsibility of driving a car. We said in so many words, "This isn't a toy, but a mode of transportation that can be be beneficial if used properly and extremely dangerous if used carelessly."

A third thing we did before the children got their licenses was talk about the virtues of defensive driving and emphasize our opinion that most accidents are preventable. We were very specific, ticking off the things involved in defensive driving. We said something like, "If a driver allows enough room between himself and the next car, goes a safe speed for the road, and is careful in changing lanes, always looking a second time before actually moving, most accidents can be avoided. The driver also needs to be constantly anticipating what the other drivers on the road might do."

We operated on the principle that people are not mind-readers, so we did not want to assume the children would know what we meant by defensive driving. We used this opportunity of riding with the children to make observations about driving practices we witnessed, road conditions and how to adjust to them, and how to safely handle the various driving situations that came up. We also made it clear that any extra premium added to our insurance because of fender-benders or other accidents would be their financial responsibility. We let them know they would be expected to pay for any tickets they might get. We also expected the children to chip in on gasoline expenses, especially when they used one of the cars for special excursions with friends. In addition, we asked them to help keep the cars looking nice, washing and cleaning them on occasion.

Supervising teenagers who are learning to drive calls for careful consideration of how things are said. This age group is particularly sensitive to criticism, so all the skills in saying things in the positive—as respectfully and non-judgmentally as possible—need to be used. When we do have to correct an action, it is important to do just that— correct the action, not the driver. We can say, "It isn't safe to turn from this lane. Move over first," not, "What are you doing, turning from this lane? You'll get us into an accident!" Anyone who expects to get into an accident probably will. We want to promote confidence rather than lack of confidence. This is another time to think how we would train an employee for a job. Positive instruction given in a respectful manner is the most productive way, and the same applies to teaching the new driver. (Please see Chapter 2.)

To reemphasize the importance of how we relate to teenagers, let me point out that it is hard for this age group, now verging on adulthood, to remain under the thumb of parents. It is hard for people of any age to be new and awkward at something. It is downright embarrassing for a teenager who is driving to be seen by friends while being supervised by a parent. I remember one incident when I was teaching our son how to parallel park. Some of his friends walked by and my son, leaning his head out the window, shouted, "I'm teaching my mommy how to park!" We all knew just what was happening, but he made light of an embarrassing situation.

It took six months for my husband to "feel comfortable" enough to allow the children to get their licenses, but the dividends were great. We were quite confident, not only of the children's ability to drive, but also of their attitudes about the responsibility they were assuming. We reemphasized this responsibility to our son when he started out on his first date after receiving his license. We reminded him that he was not only responsible for his own safety, but the precious daughter of another family. When our daughters started dating, we hoped that other parents did the same with their sons. The children were accident and violation-free through college age. In fact, when our son finally got a car of his own and applied for insurance, they asked, "How many accidents?" "None" "How many tickets?" "None." They could not believe it. No doubt there are other families' children with this same good record. It is certainly one worth striving for—for parent and teenager alike.

Every family has to figure out how it will finance a teenager's driving. Some families buy their teenager a car and pay for the insurance; others pay for the additional driver insurance on the family car. Other families expect the teenager to pay part or all of these expenses. Circumstances and rationales vary. We felt that our children would have a car of their own only when they could afford to buy and maintain it and pay for the insurance. Consequently, they did not have their own cars until after they finished college. However, we paid for adding the children to our family car insurance before that, with the understanding, as mentioned above, that they would pay for any extra premium added as a result of accidents. They also contributed some to the cost of gasoline, especially when they went on major excursions.

It was an exciting day when the children finally got their drivers' licenses. They felt as though they had received wings, and we certainly enjoyed being liberated from ferrying them everywhere. I remember with real pleasure the day we gave each of our children a set of "keys to the cars," a symbol to all of their coming of age and their being well-disciplined behind the wheel.

Handling College Expenses

Financing the children's college education is a major concern of most parents. Although it gets much more expensive all the time, as tuitions and living expenses rise, children of college age can help finance their own education to some extent. Also, the choice of an institution of learning influences the cost. State institutions are not as expensive as private ones, and community colleges can provide the first two years at a fraction of the cost.

Children can be expected to pay for part of their college expenses by working summers and saving their money for that purpose. Each family has to figure out what expenses they will cover and what they expect their college students to take care of. In our case, we agreed to pay for tuition, room and board, books, a clothing allowance, and travel to and from college. (We did not want the children to ponder whether or not they could afford to come home for a visit!) Their responsibility was to pay for incidentals, including entertainment, and any extra clothes they wanted to buy. Summer employment covered their part of the expenses nicely, and they were already used to handling their own money after years of experience receiving an allowance and managing their clothing allowance. It was also part of the general agreement that they would do their best work in college, as well as write home.

Some students want to work while going to college in order to earn more money. Although this is a worthy goal, it could make grades suffer, especially the first year or two when there are so many adjustments. We encouraged the children not to work during the first year of college, and after that, for only a few hours a week.

Education comes first, and college study takes many hours of hard work. We managed all right financially with this arrangement with two in state institutions of learning at once, and sometimes three! If expenses are too high to accomplish this nowadays, it is worth taking out a loan to avoid a student's working too many hours. Of course, grants and scholarships should be explored.

Another approach to financing a college education is to have the children work a year between high school and college and save toward the expenses. I knew a family with several children close together who did. Not only was it more possible in this way to afford college, but the children matured during that year of work and were more ready for the demands of college or university study.

Working to defray the cost of a college education has several benefits. Obviously it helps financially, and just as important, the children appreciate their education more if they are involved. It also helps them experience the real world, learn more about the value of money and its place in our way of life, and, perhaps, know better what they want to do with their education.

Financing a college education is one of the final challenges of getting through the teen years. What we are sometimes not ready for is that children need our moral, and often financial, support even after this period. The relationship we build with them during the teen years can set the tone of our relationship after they become independent adults, so it is worthy of careful nurturing.

11

THE ROLE OF GRANDPARENTS

Grandparents, too, have a role in rearing children. Involved grandparents can have a very special relationship with their grandchildren, which helps the grandchildren develop a feeling of self worth, a very important factor in promoting good behavior. Grandparents do this mainly by being those special people who think the grandchildren are wonderful, play with and read to them, and have them stay overnight on occasion. Children who have grandparents to whom they can relate get a very special sense of well-being, a real plus in their lives.

It is important, also, how we relate to our adult children so that there is a good feeling between all parties. That can be very influential in how often we see or communicate with our children and grandchildren. The same principles of attention, respect and empathy that are so important for younger children still apply. They are essential for good relationships with sons and daughters, as both children and adults.

Although attention and empathy are very important, the greatest challenge to grandparents is to *respect* their adult children. This is especially true in regard to their space, as described in the chapter on respect (Chapter 2.) It is their decision—their space—how to raise their children, what to spend their money on, or which schools to send the children to. In order to establish good relationships as grandparents, it is wise never to give advice unless asked. It is hard not to, when you think you know best or have a better idea, but it is seldom happily received, and somehow things usually work out all right without it. I make an exception, however, when it is a matter of safety. Then I speak out.

If grandparents live close enough, there is an opportunity to help their own children by baby-sitting on occasion, enjoying the grandchildren in the process. However, it is important to remember that grandparents have "space," too. The parents need to place baby-sitting requests as far in advance as possible, and not too often, unless some understanding has been reached for a regular night out or care for the grandchildren while the parents work. If grandparents feel their space is being invaded, they can give an "I" message, such as, "I'd be glad to baby-sit, but we have plans for Saturday night. Please let me know sooner so I can put it on the calendar." It is better to work out a good understanding about your conditions for baby-sitting than to have strained relations.

Another crucial issue is your standard for the grandchildren's behavior in *your* house. It is entirely different from giving unsolicited advice, because this is your space, not that of your children. The grandchildren quickly learn what is expected in each household. I have heard some people say that they hate to see their grandchildren coming because of their misbehavior. I believe people have every right to correct a child in their house, even when a parent is present if the parents do not do so. An "I" or "we" message is least likely to offend. You can say to the child, "We don't climb on tables. Here are some toys you can play with."

I learned in a grandparenting seminar that it helps grandchildren develop a feeling of belonging if they have their own place for toys in your house. It surely has worked well for us. I thought there was not space in the room where we always gather, but I managed to clear out one cabinet for toys for our oldest granddaughter when she was the only grandchild. Every time she came over she made a beeline for "her cabinet" and began to play. She had her own space in our house. Now, all four grandchildren know where the toys are. Very important, too, in making the house suitable for grandchildren, is to make it safe by putting detergent, cleaners and anything else toxic or dangerous out of reach.

On the subject of grandchildren in *our* home, we make it much easier for our children if we follow the same general guidelines the parents have set—for example, keeping the same routine for eating and bedtime and not "letting them get away with" inappropriate behavior. I do not think a slight deviation from parental expectations is harmful, however, since a visit with the grandparents is a special time and children quickly learn to expect different standards from different people. It is the major deviation that could make it hard for the parents, such as a much later bedtime or a gift at each get-together.

The joy of grandparenting can be overdone if it is the only joy in the grandparents' lives. It can result in the grandparents' wanting to spend so much time with their grandchildren that they become intrusive. It is important for all of us, especially when retired, to develop interests and friends to take the place of raising our own families and of our everyday work. There are lots of worthy organizations, church and civic as well as volunteer, that welcome and need our active participation. Like everything else, there is a happy medium in which we have our own activities but also have time for the grandchildren.

The joys of grandparenting are many, and at this point, my husband and I are just beginning to sample them. I believe that the very best way to enhance these joys and our relations with the grandchildren and their parents is to be constantly aware of their space and show respect for it.

PART FOUR

REST STOPS

12

SOME PARTING
THOUGHTS

For Late Comers: Do Not Expect Miracles

"I did just what was recommended, but still my child won't cooperate." This is a pretty typical reaction from many parents, especially if a child is a preteen or teen. Both the children and their parents may have gotten into patterns of behavior which cannot be modified overnight. It is hard for parents who are new to this approach to get all the judgmental tone and wording out of what they say. They may *think* they are using non-judgmental language, but it may be only a slight modification of the same old mode of communication. It takes a lot of practice to develop new ways. For example, in attempting to use an "I" message, a parent might say, "I think you look messy in that outfit." There is still that judgmental word "messy" in the comment, and it would be hard to escape a derogatory tone of voice. More effective might be, "It really bothers me when your clothes don't look neat and clean." Sticking to how it makes you feel while describing the actual situation will get less resistance.

As another example, if a child habitually is not ready on time, an "I" message may have the desired effect. You could say, "It really bothers me when we always have to wait for you." Then you could ask what would help her be ready at the appointed time. She may come up with a good idea. Perhaps she needs a clock in her room or help in getting her clothes in order, or maybe she needs to start getting ready sooner. Problem-solving may come up with a solution. If it continues to happen, try a logical consequence. If she is old enough to stay home alone, leave without her. In the case of a ride stopping by, encourage the driver to go on without her. All these actions need to be done in the spirit of logical consequences after you have talked about the possibility of their happening, and not as "punishment."

You will notice that in the examples above there is no attack on the person. You are only making clear your expectations for her actions. One of the hardest things for a parent to "relearn" is not to attack the child verbally. Children will either resist or wilt, neither of which you want. By keeping the focus on the situation, you inspire cooperation.

Although the method described can work well for younger children, it may not work for preteens and teens who have been regularly resisting limits and who are experiencing a great deal of peer pressure. Some real heart-to-heart talks about why you are concerned, being very careful to be *reasonable, respectful, open-minded, and non-judgmental,* are the most hopeful venues for coming to some sort of agreement. The older the child, the more she has to be the one to make the decision to modify her actions. A parent does not have much leverage except turning a child out of the home if she will not follow the family limits, and no conscientious parent wants that. The only option is good, reasoned communication. It is hard, although not impossible, to establish such communication when the child reaches her teens. Of course, it is most helpful to start good communication when the child is young and develop it over the years.

Patience, perseverance and consistency; these are essential to success. Usually you will get cooperation if you lay out expectations clearly, reasonably, *respectfully,* and then wait patiently for results. I should like to add a special word about patience— not patience with the behavior you do not want, but patience in getting the behavior you do want. Often there is a time lag in which the situation does not occur again and the child can use that time to make the decision to behave as you have outlined.

Ultimately it is the child's decision, and she usually needs time to respond to your request or to consider the logical consequences that you have indicated will follow the undesired behavior. A demand for "instant change" in behavior will likely get resistance, for the child would have the feeling of "giving in." In the case when a change in behavior is needed right away, it helps to allow for a little face-saving action, such as taking a few more minutes to get ready on a family excursion for a teenager, or one more toot on the whistle for a toddler. Often that is enough to satisfy the desire to be the decision-maker.

It may seem difficult to use the principles of preventive discipline as outlined in this book, especially when it is started late in the child's upbringing. However, it can be successful in inspiring cooperation, avoiding conflicts and developing self discipline, all worthy goals.

"Happiness Is Expecting The Possible"

In my opinion, "expecting the possible" is one of the most important concepts in getting the actions we want from our children. Two of the most crucial factors determining just what is possible are 1) the maturity and age of the child, and 2) the customs of the time.

Happiness is expecting the possible

Age and Maturity

Age and maturity relate directly to what is "possible." Most young children have a hard time sitting quietly in church (or elsewhere for that matter), waiting while the parent shops, or putting off eating and sleeping. If a child is cranky, he is most likely bored, hungry or tired. The best remedy is not to expect the impossible.

As children get older they can, of course, cope better with putting off their needs and desires. Determining when this occurs and at what rate for each child is the challenge. It is partly a matter of experimentation. If a situation is too much for an individual child, we can back off a bit, lessening the expectations and making adjustments.

We can avoid taking our children places that make unsuitable demands, being sure they can eat and sleep when necessary. We can take toys and games when we expect to wait in the doctor's office or take a long car trip. In addition, we meet the most success having well-behaved children if we do not upset their schedules. It is a matter of respect. Finally, getting a sitter when we want to go to an adult function is a good investment so that we will not make impossible demands of our children, and it has the added advantage of giving parents some time free from what amounts to a 24-hour responsibility.

Customs of the Times

We have all heard of second-generation problems in which old-country customs and mores clash with those of the adopted country. Generation to generation mores can even clash in the same country. It is helpful to examine our expectations in such matters. Are they realistic in today's world? Are they necessary for the health, safety or moral well-being of the child? If they are, we should stick by them. However, if they are "old tapes" being played from our upbringing which are not applicable to-day, we are wise to discard them.

Whenever a conflict arises between our children and us, we can examine our reactions to see if they are valid before delivering an edict. A parent can say, "Let me think about it." It saves lots of turmoil, backing down and anger—all negative reactions. We gain stature as reasonable parents and our decision is much more acceptable if we have given it careful thought, even if our final decision does not grant the original request. What comes through is that we care about our child, not only his safety and well-being, but how he feels.

A technique which I found helpful when an unsatisfactory situation arose was transactional analysis. What I understood by this imposing term was to look critically at each situation that a child did not handle well and try to figure out why, then problem-solve and plan a strategy to avoid the offending circumstances. For example, my daughter's two-year-old twins cried every time she washed their hair. Applying transactional analysis brought out the fact that they hated the water running down their faces and into their eyes. A moistened, folded wash cloth which my daughter taught the girls to hold over their eyes during the operation and toweling their wet hair right when they got out of the tub solved the problem of water in the eyes. Now, hair washing is not a problem.

In conclusion, I believe that the concept "happiness is expecting the possible" exemplifies the truly constructive use of the three elements of preventive discipline I have put forth in this book: attention, respect and empathy. It takes sensitive, positive attention to stay in tune with our children's maturity level and outlook on life, respect to work with whatever level that happens to be, and empathy not only to help each child over the rough spots but to help the parent understand what is bothering the child. As we gain this understanding, adjustments can be made to match the expectations with "the possible."

Taking seriously the importance of the "happiness is expecting the possible" concept is, I think, key to enjoying success in the multifaceted job of child-rearing. It follows that the more success we have, the more likely we are to be happy parents with happy children, a goal to which we all aspire.

APPENDIX

THE BE-ATTITUDES

Be attentive

Be positive

Be clear

Be consistent

Be non-judgmental

Be reasonable

Be open-minded

Be respectful

Be supportive

Be understanding

Be empathetic

Be loving

Be fun

FAMILY GAMES FOR TRIPS

Our family has traveled a lot, especially by car. Following are some games that have helped pass away the time and miles. For the most part, the children need to be school-age to play these games. Some preschoolers might be able to join in if the rules are modified to accommodate them. For younger children, some suitable songs or riddles would probably be better. A bookstore or the library would have books with good suggestions.

Alphabet

I imagine most everyone has played this road sign game. The object is to find the letters of the alphabet in sequence on passing signs, informing the rest of the players what letter you are on after the sign has been passed so the other players do not get extra help. The word the letter was found in does not need to be cited. The first one to get to Z is, of course, the winner. I remember that J, K, Q, X and Z were nearly always a challenge.

Boys' Names and Girls' Names

This game sounds almost too simple, but we had fun with it. If we chose boys' names, the idea was to go in rotation around the family stating a different boy's name (no foreign language). If anyone repeated a name already used or could not think of a new one, that person was out. The last one left in the game was the winner. The same rules applied for girls' names.

Twenty Questions

This game is more sophisticated, so children should likely be in the upper elementary grades or higher to play. "It" thinks of an identifiable object and says whether it is "animal, vegetable or mineral," or a combination of two categories. The others, by turns, ask questions that can be answered yes or no to try to determine the object within 20 questions. The trick is to first ask questions which determine big categories. For example, if the object is animal, a question might be, "Is it human?" If the answer is "Yes," the next question could be, "Is the person living?" A good question if the category is mineral or vegetable is, "Would it fit in my hand?" to get an idea of size. Another question might be, "Is it useful?" Ideally the questions get more and more pointed until someone has an exact idea of what it is and asks a question about a specific item, such as, "Is it the first flag of the United States?" The game is challenging and good mental exercise.

U. S. States and Capitals or Foreign Countries and Capitals

This game also assumes a good bit of knowledge. The simplest form is to name states or countries using the same rules as for the game that uses boys' names and girls' names. A more advanced version would be to name a state or country and its capital. The beauty of this game is that it can be modified according to the ages of the children, with perhaps handicaps placed on the older ones. For example, the older children could have to name both the state and its capital, while the younger ones could stay in the game by just naming the state.

What I found so valuable about these games was that while passing a good bit of time and miles, we were also enjoying the camaraderie of the family. It provided good memories and helped develop a closeness.

SUGGESTED READING

Brazelton, T. Berry, M.D. *To Listen to a Child: Understanding the Normal Problems of Growing Up.* Reading, MA: Addison-Wesley, 1992. (There are many other titles by Berry T. Brazelton.)

Driekurs, Rudolf. *Children: The Challenge.* New York: Hawthorne Books, 1964.

Faber, Adele, and Elaine Mazlish. *How to Talk so Kids Will Listen and Listen so Kids Will Talk.* New York: Rawson, Wade Publisher, Inc., 1980.

Ginott, Haim. *Between Parent and Child.* New York: Avon, 1982.

Gordon, Thomas. *Parent Effective Training: The Tested New Way to Raise Responsible Children.* New York: NAL-Dutton, 1975.

Ilg, Frances, M.D., Louise Ames, Ph.D., Sidney Baker, M.D. Child Behavior: *The classic child care manual from the Gesell Institute of Human Development.* New York: Harper Perennial, 1992. (There is also a book for each age of development from ages two to ten by Louise Ames.)

Nelson, Jane, Ed.D. *Positive Discipline.* New York: Ballantine Books, 1981.

Spock, Benjamin, M.D., and Michael Rothenburg. *Baby and Child Care,* 6th revised edition. New York: Dutton, 1992.

Additional copies of

PREVENTIVE DISCIPLINE
by Janice S. Barnhart

may be ordered by sending
a check or money order for $9.95
plus $2.00 shipping
(California residents add sales tax to $9.95)

to

Janice S. Barnhart
P. O. Box 5120
San Mateo, CA 94403

Same shipping and handling for
up to and including 9 copies.
Quantity discounts for 10 or more are available.